Structures of Subjectivity

Psychoanalytic Inquiry Book Series

Volume 4

Psychoanalytic Inquiry
Book Series

Vol. 1: *Reflections on Self Psychology*–*Joseph D. Lichtenberg &*
Samuel Kaplan (eds.)

Vol. 2: *Psychoanalysis and Infant Research*–*Joseph D. Lichtenberg*

Vol. 4: *Structures of Subjectivity: Explorations in Psychoanalytic*
Phenomenology–*George E. Atwood & Robert D. Stolorow*

Vol. 5: *Towards a Comprehensive Model for Schizophrenic Disorders:*
Psychoanalytic Essays in Memory of Ping-Nie Pao, M.D.
–*David B. Feinsilver*

Vol. 6 & 7: *The Borderline Patient: Emerging Concepts in Diagnosis,*
Psychodynamics, and Treatment, 1 & 2–*James S. Grotstein,*
Marion F. Solomon, & Joan A. Lang (eds.)

Vol. 8: *Psychoanalytic Treatment: An Intersubjective Approach*
–*Robert D. Stolorow, Bernard Brandchaft, & George E. Atwood*

Vol. 9: *Female Homosexuality: Choice Without Volition*–*Elaine V. Siegel*

Vol. 10: *Psychoanalysis and Motivation*–*Joseph D. Lichtenberg*

Vol. 11: *Cancer Stories: Creativity and Self-Repair*
–*Esther Dreifuss-Kattan*

Vol. 12: *Contexts of Being: The Intersubjective Foundations of*
Psychological Life–*Robert D. Stolorow & George E. Atwood*

Vol. 13: *Self and Motivational Systems: Toward a Theory of*
Psychoanalytic Technique–*Joseph D. Lichtenberg, Frank M. Lachmann, &*
James L. Fosshage

Structures of Subjectivity

Explorations in
Psychoanalytic Phenomenology

George E. Atwood
Robert D. Stolorow

THE ANALYTIC PRESS

1984   Hillsdale, NJ   London

The Analytic Press
365 Broadway
Hillsdale, New Jersey 07642

Library of Congress Cataloging-in-Publication Data

Atwood, George E.
  Structures of subjectivity.

  (Psychoanalytic inquiry book series; v. 4)
  Bibliography: p.
  Includes indexes.
  1. Psychoanalysis. 2. Phenomenological psychology.
3. Existential psychology. 4. Subjectivity–
Psychological aspects I. Stolorow, Robert D.
II. Title. III. Series. [DNLM: 1. Psychoanalytic
theory. W1 PS427F v.4 / WM 460 A887s]
BF173.A75 1984   616.89′17   83-15873
ISBN 0-88163-166-3

First paperback edition 1993

Printed in the United States of America
10 9 8 7 6 5

To Ben, Lisa, Rebecca, and Stephie

Contents

Preface   ix

1. **Philosophical Context and Basic Concepts**   1

   The Hermeneutic Tradition   2
     The Psychoanalytic Case Study   4
   Existential Phenomenology   7
   Structuralism   31
     Personality Structure   33
     Motivation   35
     Repression and the Unconscious   35
     Personality Development   36
     Psychological Health and Pathology   39

2. **Intersubjectivity: I. The Therapeutic Situation**   41

   The Psychoanalytic Situation   42
   Transference and Countertransference   47
   Negative Therapeutic Reactions   52
   Psychopathology   55
   Therapeutic Action   59
   Conclusions   63

3. Intersubjectivity: II. Development and
    Pathogenesis   65

    Self-Object Differentiation   71
    Integration of Affectively Discrepant
        Experiences   76
    The Passing of the Oedipal Period   79
    Conclusions   83

4. Pathways of Concretization   85

    Neurotic Symptoms   86
    Symbolic Objects   88
    Enactments   91
    Dreams   97
    Conclusions   116

5. Concluding Remarks   119

References   121

Author Index   127

Subject Index   129

Preface

This book is the product of a ten-year collaboration, bringing together several lines of interest, including the psychology of knowledge and the subjective origins of psychological theory (Stolorow & Atwood, 1979), the desire to reframe psychoanalysis as pure psychology (Klein, 1976; Kohut, 1977), and an abiding commitment to understanding the invariant structures of experience that organize personal, subjective worlds. From the confluence of these interests crystallized a vision of a psychoanalytic phenomenology devoted to the illumination of meanings in personal experience and conduct. The chapters that follow can be seen as a progress report on our ongoing efforts to actualize this vision of a psychoanalytic science of human subjectivity.

One of us (G.E.A.) wishes to acknowledge the profound influence of the teachings of Silvan Tomkins. The other (R.D.S.) acknowledges the deep impact of the inspirational work of the late Heinz Kohut. Bernard Brandchaft, in addition to coauthoring chapter 3, contributed importantly to the evolution of the ideas in chapter 2. Certain of the ideas in the section on therapeutic action in chapter 2 were originally formulated with the collaboration of John Munder Ross. We wish to thank Frank Lachmann and Richard Ulman for providing us with clinical illustrations and for their stimulating discussions of our work, and Beatrice Beebe for helping to guide us through the literature on infant observation and for her valuable suggestions regarding chapter 3. Among the many students and colleagues who have helped us to sharpen our ideas, we wish to give special mention to Elizabeth Atwood, Virginia Stolorow, Barbara Blum, Michael Gara, Arnold Goldberg, Chris Jaenicke, Claudia Kohner, Peter Lessem, Dorthy Levinson, Etienne Perold, Louis Petrillo, Kathie Ramsland, Emanuel Shapiro, Thomas Smith, Dede Socarides, Marian Tolpin, Ernest Wolf, and Peter Zimmermann.

Some of the material in this book was originally published in the following books and journals: *Faces in a Cloud,* R. Stolorow and G. Atwood (N.Y.: Jason Aronson, 1979); *Psychoanalysis of Developmental Arrests,* R. Stolorow and F. Lachmann (N.Y.: International Universities Press, 1980); *The Future of Psychoanalysis,* ed. A. Goldberg (N.Y.: International Universities Press, 1983, pp. 3-16); *The International Review of Psycho-Analysis* (1978, 5:247-256 and 313-320); *The International Journal of Psycho-Analysis* (1979, 60:39-45); *Psychoanalysis and Contemporary Thought* (1980, 3:267-290); *Bulletin of the Menninger Clinic* (1981, 45:20-28 and 1983, 47:117-128); *Contemporary Psychoanalysis* (1981, 17:197-208); *The Annual of Psychoanalysis* (1982, 10:205-220); and *The Psychoanalytic Review* (1983, 70: 143-162). We thank the editors and publishers of these books and journals for giving us permission to include this material in our book.

And finally, we wish to express our gratitude to Lawrence Erlbaum and Joseph Lichtenberg for their support of this project.

George E. Atwood
Robert D. Stolorow

Structures of Subjectivity

1   PHILOSOPHICAL CONTEXT AND BASIC CONCEPTS

This book brings together a series of efforts to rethink the conceptual and methodological foundations of psychoanalytic theory. These efforts have been guided by three general considerations. First, we have felt that any new framework should be capable of preserving the contributions made by the classical analytic theorists and of translating these contributions into a common conceptual language. Second, it is our view that the theory of psychoanalysis should be formulated on an experience-near level of discourse, closely anchored in the phenomena of clinical observation. The third guiding consideration is found in our belief that an adequate theory of personality must be designed to illuminate the structure, significance, origins, and therapeutic transformations of personal subjective worlds in all their richness and diversity. The intellectual heritage upon which we have drawn in fashioning our "psychoanalytic phenomenology" is a very broad one, embracing the hermeneutic tradition in the philosophy of history, aspects of the existential-phenomenological movement, basic concepts of modern structuralism, and certain trends in contemporary Freudian thought which have in common the notion that psychoanalysis should be reframed as pure psychology. In the sections that follow, we discuss these various influences and give a sketch of our view of the nature of psychoanalytic investigation and knowledge.

THE HERMENEUTIC TRADITION

Psychoanalytic phenomenology is a depth psychology of human subjectivity devoted to the illumination of meanings in personal experience and conduct. It may thus be grouped with what the German philosopher-historian Wilhelm Dilthey (1926) called the *Geisteswissenschaften* or human sciences. According to Dilthey, the human sciences are to be distinguished from the sciences of nature because of a fundamental difference in attitude toward their respective objects of investigation: The natural sciences investigate objects from the outside whereas the human sciences rely on a perspective from the inside. The supreme category of the human sciences is that of *meaning,* which is something that exists within human subjectivity rather than on the plane of material nature. The central emphasis in the natural sciences, as Dilthey viewed them, was upon causal explanation; the task of inquiry in the human sciences, by contrast, he saw as interpretation and understanding. Understanding (*Verstehen*) denotes the act by which one passes from the sign to the thing signified, from the expression to the meaning being expressed. This focus on interpretation and understanding was part of an overall conception of the methodology of human sciences as essentially *hermeneutic* in character. Hermeneutics is the theory of interpretation originally developed by scholars of religion seeking to understand and explicate the meaning of Scriptural writings. After it was expanded by Schleiermacher to apply to any literary text, Dilthey further elaborated hermeneutics into a tool for interpreting human history in general.

Dilthey argued that understanding of historical events is achieved through a process of "re-experiencing" (Makkreel, 1975, p. 252). This means that the historian must reconstruct the world of meaning belonging to an event and then comprehend that world from the viewpoint of its own intrinsic structure. This process closely resembles the interpretive analysis of texts and follows a pattern known as the "hermeneutic circle." In textual interpretation, the meaning of a particular passage is established primarily by considerations relating the passage to the structure of the text as a whole; parts of the work are thus assessed in relation to an understanding of the totality while knowledge of the whole is constituted by study of the parts. Dilthey characterized historical inquiry as involving a similarly circular movement between a focus on particular events and a view of the total meaning-context in which those events participate.

One of the consequences of adopting a hermeneutic approach in the human studies is the recognition that the knowing subject is one with the object of knowledge: both are human individuals. This identity of subject and object is responsible for a distinctive feature of the methodology of these disciplines: the investigator can, indeed *must* draw upon his own experience and self-knowledge to guide his interpretations of the lives of those he studies. Dilthey made this link between subject and object explicit in his definition of the mode of insight established in the human sciences as "the rediscovery of the I in the Thou" (1926, p. 191). This bond of kinship uniting the investigator with his subject matter is also responsible for a particular difficulty in the human sciences: the investigator is an experiencing individual, situated personally and historically, and his quest for knowledge is accordingly subject to the influence of all those historical, personal, and circumstantial factors that come into play in every human action. These factors inevitably relativize the investigator's understanding and threaten to subvert the aim of arriving at conclusions possessing general validity. Dilthey's solution to the apparent antithesis between the historical-situational relativity of human understanding and the striving for universal knowledge was to propose a "critique of historical reason." This he envisioned as an analysis devoted to rendering conscious and explicit the finite existential perspectives associated with all inquiry in the human sciences.

Dilthey's insights and proposals have given rise to a broad hermeneutic tradition radiating outward from the philosophy of history to influence thinking in all the disciplines concerned with understanding human existence (Palmer, 1969; Gadamer, 1975).

This tradition has a special significance for psychoanalysis, which in spite of being an interpretive science in its methods and goals, has since its inception been encumbered by a felt obligation to ground itself on natural science concepts. The notion that psychoanalysis is a hermeneutic or historical discipline rather than a natural science has been persuasively argued by Lacan (1953), Sherwood (1969), Ricouer (1970), and more recently Steele (1979) and Leavy (1980). This idea is also implicit in the radical proposals for psychoanalytic theory made by Guntrip (1967), Klein (1976), Schafer (1976), and Kohut (1977), all of whom reject the mechanistic language of Freudian metapsychology in favor of experience-near concepts addressed to the realms of personal meaning and personal action. This book as well represents a further effort to develop the implications of the hermeneutic viewpoint for psychoanalysis.

One group of issues to which hermeneutic considerations are particularly germane concerns our conception of the nature of psychoanalytic investigation. In the next section we discuss these issues with specific emphasis on the individual case study, the problem of validation of interpretations, and the intersubjective field in which psychoanalytic understanding is generated.

The Psychoanalytic Case Study

The individual case study has been and seems assured of remaining the central method by which psychoanalytic knowledge is advanced. How is an understanding of a person's life established in a case study? All psychoanalytic understanding is interpretive understanding, in the sense that it always entails a grasp of the meaning of something that has been expressed. This meaning belongs to an individual's personal subjective world and becomes accessible to understanding in the medium of the analyst's empathy. Empathy arises as a possibility in the case study because of the common bond of humanity shared by the observer and the observed. The inquiry concerns an experiencing person, who stands in turn within the experiential field of the analyst, and empathy is implicit in the attempt to understand a person's communications and actions from the standpoint of his own subjective frame of reference (Kohut, 1959).

The development of psychoanalytic understanding may be conceptualized as an intersubjective process[1] involving a dialogue between two personal universes. The goal of this dialogue is the illumination of the inner pattern of a life, that distinctive structure of meanings that connects the different parts of an individual's world into an intelligible whole. The actual conduct of a psychoanalytic case study comprises a series of empathic inferences into the structure of an individual's subjective life, alternating and interacting with the analyst's acts of reflection upon the involvement of his own personal reality in the ongoing investigation. Every such study begins in a modest way, with a single instance of a person's behavior. One or more interpretive hypotheses are posed regarding the experiential and life-historical context within which that behavior has meaning. The analyst then studies further instances of the individual's communications and actions and poses further hypotheses about the subjective and genetic contexts to which they belong. In this way a field of provisionally identified meanings comes into existence, and these meanings are compared and cross-linked, with the validity of any particular insight concerning the person being assessed by its degree of coherence with the analysis as a whole. The interplay between individual hypotheses and the analysis as a totality follows a "hermeneutic circle," in which the parts give rise to the whole and the whole provides a context for evaluation of the parts. The structures of meaning disclosed by this mode of investigation become manifest in invariant thematic configurations that are repeated in different sectors of the person's experiences. The elucidation of such invariants forms the counterpart in the interpretive science of psychoanalysis to the doctrine of replication of observations in the sciences of nature.

Since psychoanalytic case studies are interpretive procedures throughout, the validity of their results is evaluated in light of distinctively hermeneutic criteria. These criteria include the log-

---

[1]Lacan (1953) and Duncan (1981), writing from theoretical vantage points differing from ours, also use the term "intersubjective" to characterize the nature of psychoanalytic understanding. Leavy (1980), drawing on the work of Lacan, advances a viewpoint broadly similar to ours, arguing that psychoanalytic understanding is reached through a process of dialogue shaped by the personal world and history of both participants.

ical coherence of the argument, the comprehensiveness of the explanation, the consistency of the interpretations with accepted psychological knowledge, and the aesthetic beauty of the analysis in disclosing previously hidden patterns of order in the material being investigated.

The varied patterns of meaning that emerge in psychoanalytic research are brought to light within a specific psychological field located at the point of intersection of two subjectivities. Because the dimensions and boundaries of this field are intersubjective in nature, the interpretive conclusions of every case study must, in a very profound sense, be understood as *relative* to the intersubjective context of their origin. The intersubjective field of a case study is generated by the interplay between transference and countertransference; it is the environment or "analytic space" (Viderman, 1974) in which the various hypotheses of the study crystallize, and it defines the horizons of meaning within which the truth-value of the final interpretations is determined. An appreciation of this dependence of psychoanalytic insight on a particular intersubjective interaction helps us to understand why the results of a case study may vary as a function of the person conducting it. Such variation, an anathema to the natural sciences, occurs because of the diverse perspectives of different investigators on material displaying an inherent plurality of meanings. The analyst is aware of the nature of interpretation as "the rediscovery of the I in the Thou" (Dilthey) and therefore knows that each of his ideas is grounded in and limited by the finite perspectives of his own personal world. This capacity for critical self-reflection opens his thinking to alternative conceptions and establishes the possibility of integrating his interpretations with ideas developed from differently situated points of view.

A psychoanalytic explanation is generally communicated to others in the form of a narrative case history, written to display the various details of a person's life as expressions of unifying themes or patterns. It is required of this narrative account that it be internally self-consistent and capable of being followed in its own terms, a feature which derives from the status of psychoanalysis as an essentially historical discipline, committed to the narrative mode of truth (Sherwood, 1969; Ricouer, 1974; Gallie,

1974; Spence, 1982). But psychoanalytic histories must go beyond fulfilling the requirements of the narrative and accomplish something further; they must bridge the gulf between the concrete particularity of an individual life and the experience of being human in universal terms. The task of writing a psychoanalytic narrative is one of transposing the analyst's understanding into a presentation illuminating the life under study for the intellectual community at large. This means unveiling the experiences of that life in a form to which others can relate their own personal worlds in empathic dialogue. The intersubjective field of the analysis serves a mediating function in this regard, providing the initial basis of comparison for describing the pattern of the individual's life as the realization of shared human possibilities.

EXISTENTIAL PHENOMENOLOGY

The point of departure for psychoanalytic phenomenology is the concept of an experiencing subject. This means that at the deepest level of our theoretical constructions we are operating within a sphere of subjectivity, abjuring assumptions that reduce experience to a material substrate. The material world, from our standpoint, is regarded as a domain of experience, and the concepts of natural science are understood as modes of organizing that domain of experience. This is in contrast to a theoretical position that would assign ontological priority to physical matter and interpret human consciousness as a secondary expression of material events. The development of knowledge in the sciences of nature involves the organizing and interconnecting of human observations, which are experiences; but materialism is a doctrine based on *reifying* the concepts of natural science and then seeing consciousness as an epiphenomenon of those reifications.

The notion that a genuine science of human experience requires its own unique concepts and methods and cannot rely on emulating the sciences of nature forms a central tenet of the existential-phenomenological movement. We are in agreement with this tenet, and especially with the phenomenological critique of doctrines of consciousness that descend from Lockean empiricism. Such doctrines rest upon a view of man as the passive receptor of discrete, atomic impressions from the outer world, an idea that body and mind are separate yet causally connected entities, and an interpretation of the nature of consciousness as a quasi-spatial container. These assumptions and metaphors involve a projection *into* experience of the qualities of material objects *of* experience, and reflect a failure to confront the attributes of subjectivity in their own distinctive terms.

Although psychoanalytic phenomenology joins with the existential-phenomenological movement in affirming the need for an autonomous science of experience, there is an important difference between the psychoanalytic approach and the phenomenological systems elaborated within philosophy. Psychoanalytic phenomenology is guided by observations conducted in the dialogue of the psychoanalytic situation, observations always made as part of an inquiry into the experiential world of a particular person. The phenomenological investigations of philosophers, by contrast, have traditionally relied on a method of solitary reflection and have inevitably defocused the individualization of a world in the quest for knowledge of subjectivity in universal terms.

As a way of defining the relationship between psychoanalytic and philosophical phenomenology in more specific terms, we shall now turn to a discussion of the systematic formulations of three important figures in the existential-phenomological movement: Edmund Husserl, Martin Heidegger, and Jean-Paul Sartre. The systems developed by these philosophers represent proposals for the understanding of human experience. By critically evaluating these proposals, we hope to bring the assumptions underlying our own thinking more clearly into view.

Edmund Husserl

Edmund Husserl conceived phenomenology as the fundamental descriptive science of human experience. Drawing inspiration from the philosophical studies of Descartes and Kant, Husserl sought to devise a method by which he could reach indubitably certain knowledge of the primordial nature of consciousness as such. The research program he proposed for this purpose, so-

called "transcendental phenomenology," was designed to elucidate the invariant structures of subjectivity that constitute the
ultimate conditions of the possibility of all conscious experience.
Because of its concern with the preconditions of all conceivable
experience, transcendental phenomenology was regarded by
Husserl as a discipline more fundamental than the traditional
empirical sciences.

The Husserlian system was understood by its founder as the
fulfillment of an historical teleology aiming toward the clarification of the foundational source of all formations of knowledge.
This source he saw in the "I-myself," the knowing subject or
"ego," which stands related to a *world* of which it is conscious.
Whereas traditional sciences take the existence of the world for
granted as a "pregiven" reality, transcendental phenomenology
suspends or "brackets" assumptions regarding the nature of objective reality and studies instead the world's manifestation to
consciousness as pure phenomenon. The procedure by which this
suspension of belief occurs is known as the phenomenological reduction or "epochē." The reduction is a mental operation by
which the phenomenologist frees himself from presuppositions
and moves into a perspective from which what had previously
been taken as real presents itself purely as a field of appearances.
The status of the world as an object of consciousness has thus
been *reduced* by the withholding of assumptions regarding its validity, nature, history, etc., and the investigator refocuses his attention on the manner of the world's givenness within his own
awareness. Husserl thought of the epochē as something utterly
without precedent in the history of science and philosophy.

> We perform the epochē . . . as a transformation of . . . the natural
> attitude of human existence which, in its total historicity, in life
> and science, was never before interrupted (1936, p. 151).[2]

The carrying out of the phenomenological reduction is said to
result in the disclosure of the pure essence that invests the world

---

[2]All references in the section on Husserl, unless otherwise indicated, are from the
book he considered the best introduction to his thought: *The Crisis of the European Sciences and Transcendental Phenomenology* (1936).

with all its meaning and validity: the transcendental ego. This is not the empirical or concrete ego of everyday life; on the contrary, the transcendental ego is understood as an entity that constitutes the meaning of existence and is ultimately responsible for defining the empirical ego and its relations to the world. Through the operation of bracketing the world and thereby reducing its status to that of a mere "correlate" of consciousness, the power of the transcendental ego in determining the features of empirical experience is brought into view.

> the world is the totality of what is taken for granted as verifiable; it is there through an aiming and is the ground for ever new aimings at what is . . . . In the epoché, however, we go back to the subjectivity which ultimately aims, which . . . has the world through previous aims and their fulfillment; and we go back to the ways in which this subjectivity . . . "has brought about," and continues to shape the world through its concealed internal "method" (p. 177).

Having uncovered transcendental subjectivity by means of the epoché, the reflections of the phenomenologist are directed toward a realm bearing little resemblance to that of ordinary empirical existence. This is a realm in which all the concrete individual features of subjective life are defocused and the universal invariants or "eidetic essences" of experience are made manifest in their stead.

Husserl metaphorically describes the epoché as the liberation of consciousness from a state of bondage:

> it is through this abstention [of the epoché] that the gaze of the philosopher in truth first becomes fully free; above all, free of the strongest and most universal, and at the same time most hidden, internal bond, namely, of the pregivenness of the world. Given in and through this liberation is the discovery of the universal, absolutely self-enclosed and absolutely self-sufficient . . . conscious life of the subjectivity which effects the validity of the world, the subjectivity which always has the world in its enduring acquisitions and continues activity to shape it anew (p. 151).

The freeing of transcendental subjectivity from immersion in the natural world has the additional effect of isolating the phenomenologist from commerce with his fellow human beings. Indeed, the whole research program of transcendental phenomenology is designed to be carried out in methodological solitude.

> The epochē creates a unique sort of philosophical solitude which is the fundamental requirement for a truly radical philosophy (p. 184).
> The radical and perfect reduction leads to the *absolutely single* ego of the pure psychologist who absolutely isolates himself and as such no longer has validity for himself as a human being or as really existing in the world but is instead the pure subject of his intentionality (p. 256).

According to Husserl, the epochē makes it apparent that the world of which we are aware manifests itself as also having existence for other subjects. The transcendental ego of the phenomenologist thus discovers itself as only one in an indefinitely large collection of other transcendental egos, all conscious of a common world. Such a formulation of *inter*subjectivity at the ground of awareness would seem to contradict the otherwise relentless emphasis on singularity and isolation. The contradiction is only apparent, however, for in the final stage of the reduction the existence of other minds is itself shown to be "constituted" by the singular action of the phenomenologist's pure subjectivity.

> it is wrong, methodically, to jump immediately into transcendental intersubjectivity and to leap over the primal "I," the ego of my epochē, which can never lose its uniqueness and personal indeclinability . . . . The epochē can show how the always singular "I," in the original constituting life proceeding within it, constitutes a first sphere of objects, the "primordial" sphere; how it then, starting from this, in a motivated fashion, performs a constitutive accomplishment through which an intentional modification of itself and its primordiality achieves ontic validity under the title of "alien-perception," perception of others, of another "I" who is for himself an "I" as I am (p. 185).

The transcendental ego of Husserlian phenomenology, subsisting in a region of irreducible subjectivity, is endowed with the remarkable power to actually *produce* the concrete empirical world in which human beings spend their lives. He who escapes the closed bondage of the natural attitude and journeys into this strange region experiences an absolute self-sufficiency and returns to the ordinary world as one transformed:

> As a phenomenologist I can, of course, at any time go back into the natural attitude, back to the straightforward pursuit of my theoretical or other life interests; I can, as before, be active as a father, a citizen, an official, as a "good European," etc., that is, as a human being in my human community, in my world. As before—and yet not quite as before . . . . Now I know that I, the previously naive ego, was none other than the transcendental ego in the mode of naive hiddenness; I know that to me, as the ego again straightforwardly perceived as a human being, there belongs inseparably a reverse side which *constitutes* and thus *really first produces* my full concreteness" (p. 210, italics added).

Psychoanalysis would be seen by the transcendental phenomenologist as operating within the "thesis of the natural standpoint" (1931, p. 91), and hence would not be regarded as a truly fundamental science. Psychoanalysis takes the existence of the world for granted and conceives of its studies in terms of a community of scholars having a shared history and shared goals. In addition, the method of psychoanalytic research relies on the dialogue, a process rendered impossible by the isolating effect of the phenomenological reduction. Husserl characterizes the reduction as a movement from preoccupation with the individual and concrete to contemplation of the universal and a priori. This movement destroys that which is of greatest significance in the psychoanalytic investigation of subjectivity; namely, the specific detail of an individual person's experience of the world. It is our view that the interpretive study of such detail in the intersubjective context of the psychoanalytic situation forms the essence of psychoanalytic research.

A central difficulty in Husserl's proposals for a science of experience pertains to a lack of clarity in his writings about the standpoint from which the research of transcendental phenomenology is conducted. The radical alteration of perspective inhering in the epoché supposedly converts the phenomenologist into a "purely theoretical spectator" (p. 298) of the structures of subjectivity that constitute the ultimate conditions of the possibility of all conscious experience. Is not the act of reflecting on these structures itself a species of experience? If it is, how can this reflection stand outside the preconditions of all experience? The project of transcendental phenomenology seems to involve an implicit goal of stepping outside the bounds of human subjectivity into a realm of presuppositionless certainty regarding the nature and function of consciousness. The notion that a single investigator can disengage himself from involvement in the world and uncover through his own isolated reflections the foundational structures of experience implies a denial of human finiteness and moreover a forgetting that human knowledge is throughout a *social* creation. We would argue in addition that the suspension of belief in the objective reality of the world places the project of transcendental phenomenology in contradiction with itself, for what of all the unsuspended presuppositions contained within the investigator's intention to carry out scientific research? Is any form of scientific work intelligible which does not at every stage view its own reason for being in terms of the human community from which it springs and the shared traditions to which it contributes?

The practice of transcendental phenomenology presents a spectacle of thought detached from social life, circling inwardly upon itself and mistaking a reified symbol of its own solitude for the discovery of its absolute foundation. The transcendental ego—that radically isolated entity disclosed in relation to a world that has been reduced to a mere correlate of its inner intentions—is thus a secondary product of the method followed in phenomenological research rather than the genuine basis of consciousness Husserl was seeking.

It is interesting to us that the radical autonomy and solitude ascribed by Husserl to the transcendental ego was closely paralleled by his personal solitude and autonomy in developing his philosophical ideas. The historian of phenomenology, H. Spiegelberg (1976), has noted how this parallelism sheds light on what otherwise might appear quite paradoxical; namely, that a philosophy aiming to become a science and encourage progress through cooperative enterprise as in other sciences failed in this endeavor almost from the outset.

His thinking was fundamentally a monologue, even when he con-
fronted merely an intimate group. At times he tried to break
through the ring of his own ideas. Thus he assigned to his private
assistant . . . the role to act as his opponent, comparable to the
"devil's advocate" in the proceedings for the canonization of a
saint. But ultimately even in such attempts to "philosophize together" he always remained his only partner (1976, pp. 88–89).

According to Spiegelberg's account, fruitful discussion was
next to impossible in Husserl's presence, even in the early days of
his teaching. He spoke in irresistible monologues, and the questions and suggestions of students and colleagues, far from having
any independent value for him, he used "merely as stimulants to
set the wheels of his own thought in ceaseless motion"
(Spiegelberg, 1976, p. 90). The final result of this exclusive preoccupation with his own thinking was that the founder of phenomenology ended his career in an almost tragic isolation, bereft of fol-
lowers, an isolation that Hussel reportedly compared with that of
a solipsist (Spiegelberg, 1976, p. 88).

There is a fundamental ambivalence in the image of consciousness that emerges from Husserlian philosophy. On the one hand,
consciousness is dominated by the one-sided closure of the natural attitude. This is an attitude in which the subject is completely
bound by interests and tasks that are directed toward the world of
objects surrounding the self. On the other hand, consciousness
may undertake the phenomenological reduction and free itself
from this natural world. In this case, subjectivity neutralizes the
binding power of objects and returns to its own inmost essence.
Husserl describes this movement as the attainment of an ideal of
independence and self-sufficiency.

Only when the spirit returns from its naive external orientation to
itself, and remains with itself and purely with itself, can it be sufficient unto itself (p. 297).

The twin tendencies of consciousness toward and away from
engagement with the objective world are interestingly mirrored
by a duality in Husserl's personal style of relating himself to others. In a letter to his teacher Franz Brentano, he described how
one part of his nature yearned to be led by others in an attitude of

reverent submission (corresponding to the bondage of the natural attitude), while another part was ruthlessly critical and obliged him always to free himself from the influence of others and follow his own independent pathway (corresponding to the liberation of the transcendental reduction).

> Probably no other urge in my constitution is more developed than that to revere, to follow those whom I love reverently, and to take their side with eagerness. But as my nature unfortunately has two sides, there is also in me an indomitable critical sense which, unconcerned about my emotional inclinations, analyzes cooly and rejects ruthlessly what appears to it untenable. Thus bound by sentiment, free by intellect, I pursue my course with scant happiness. Always inclined to acknowledge the superiority of others and to let them lead me upward, again and again I find myself compelled to part company with them and to seek my own way (quoted in Spiegelberg, 1976, p. 89).

Husserl's emphasis on the solitude of the epoché and the isolation of the transcendental ego appears to us to have been linked with a personal need to detach himself from others and consolidate a sense of his own intellectual autonomy. While the presence of such a linkage in no way invalidates Husserlian phenomenology, we would suggest that it does illuminate a facet of his thought in which he alone believed. By defining the reduction as the central method of phenomenological research and by grounding his ideas on the concept of the transcendental ego, Husserl effectively isolated himself from others and eliminated the possibility of genuine progress in his new science of experience.

Martin Heidegger

Heidegger's contributions to phenomenology were made in the context of his life-long quest for understanding of the meaning of being. Unlike Husserl, whose central fascination was with the knowing subject or ego, Heidegger's explorations circle around the problem of unveiling the nature of being as such. His magnum opus, *Being and Time* (1927)[3], is an attempt to prepare the

---

[3]All references in the discussion of Heidegger are from this work.

way for an understanding of being in general by clarifying the nature of a particular being—Man. Heidegger's analyses deal with the ontology of the person and are therefore relevant to a discussion of the assumptions underlying psychoanalysis as a human science.

Heidegger refers to the mode of being belonging to a person as "Dasein" (being-there). He justifies the selection of Dasein as the proper approach to universal ontology by noting that there is a special relationship between the question of being and Dasein's essential nature.

> Dasein is an entity which does not just occur among other entities. Rather it is . . . distinguished by the fact that, in its very Being, that Being is an *issue* for it (p. 32).
> Dasein always understands itself in terms of a possibility of itself: to be itself or not itself (p. 33).

Concern with the issue of being defines both the sovereign theme of *Being and Time* and also the central distinguishing characteristic of Dasein. Heidegger's book displays an interesting relationship to itself in this connection: Its portrait of man is a microcosm of the work itself, a sketch-in-miniature mirroring the concerns that motivate the philosophy as a whole. The inquiry into the nature of being, by defining Man as an entity for which being is an issue, posits its own ontological motivation as the essence of being human.

The issue of being is a deeply problematic one in the world of Heidegger's thought, for at the heart of Dasein's nature lies a tendency to interpret its own being on the model of objects other than itself.

> Dasein gets its ontological understanding of itself in the first instance from those entities which it itself is *not* but which it encounters "within" its world, and from the Being which they possess (p. 85).

It is inherent in Dasein, according to Heidegger, to have a mistaken self-conception, to envision itself as something which in actuality it is not. In noting this self-estrangement, he claims to have identified one of Man's deepest ontological attributes.

The kind of Being which belongs to Dasein is . . . such that, in understanding its Being, it has a tendency to do so in terms of that
entity toward which it comports itself proximally—in terms of the
"world" (p. 86).

Substantial portions of *Being and Time* are devoted to
explicating the attributes of Dasein in such a manner as to
sharply distinguish it from the kinds of entities encountered in
its world. Heidegger uses the term "existentialia" to refer to these
attributes, differentiating them from the properties possessed by
objects, which he calls "categories." His analysis thus runs in a
direction counter to Dasein's inclination to fall back upon its
world and interpret itself in terms of that world. *Being and Time*
circles reflexively on itself, in that the questioning of Dasein's being is itself explicitly taken as one of Dasein's modes of being.
This book may therefore be understood as an effort *by* Dasein to
separate itself from the world and assemble a representation of
its own distinctive selfhood.

The existentialia discussed by Heidegger form a system of interlocking "ontological structural concepts" referring to the a
priori foundation of human existence. He arrives at these
through an analysis of Dasein as it is seen in its concrete actuality or everydayness. The general term under which the
existentialia fall is "being-in-the-world," where the hyphenation
emphasizes the presence of an indissociable unity. This unity is
meant to undercut the split between subject and object that has
been traditional in Western philosophical thought. Being-in-the-
world is characterized primarily in terms of that which it is not.
Being-in-the-world is *not* the mode of being of entities other than
Dasein; being-in is *not* a matter of one thing being inside another
in physical space; and the world of being-in-the-world is *not* itself
any kind of entity analogous to those Dasein encounters in its
daily life. The worldhood of the world consists in its being the irreducible context that makes it possible for entities to show themselves and be encountered. The world is thus actually a property
of Dasein's being, which is said to "have" a world.

Dasein is ontologically related to other entities by the attitude
of care (Sorge). This kind of relatedness, involving human concern and meaning, is of an altogether different order from the

mode of relatedness or interaction shown by things. Heidegger discusses two specific ways in which non-human objects are experienced: readiness-to-hand (Zuhandenheit) and presence-to-hand (Vorhandenheit). The former of these refers, broadly speaking, to man's relationship to tools or instruments, i.e., objects encountered as subordinate means to reach intended goals. The latter pertains to objects seen in a way detached from pragmatic activity and refers to the mode of theoretical contemplation.

Being-in-the-world also involves what Heidegger calls "thrownness" (Geworfenheit), meaning that Dasein finds itself in a time and a place, in circumstances not entirely of its own choosing, delivered over to a situation that possesses an enveloping "thereness" or facticity. The world into which Dasein has been thrown includes not just the kinds of entities encountered as ready-to-hand and present-to-hand; also given as a constitutive element of the human situation is the existence of other Daseins. In Heidegger's thought, there is no isolated "I" or ego such as the one which appears in Husserl's analysis of transcendental subjectivity. Being-in-the-world is inherently and indissociably a being-with-others. The attribute of being-with is described as another of the existentialia, and Heidegger again takes care to distinguish this characteristic from the kind of co-existence possessed by things in the realm of the present-at-hand.

> The phenomenological assertion that "Dasein is essentially Being-with" has an existential-ontological meaning. It does not seek to establish ontically that factically I am not present-at-hand alone, and that others of my kind occur . . . . Being-with is an existential characteristic of Dasein even when factically no Other is present at-hand or perceived. Even Dasein's Being-alone is Being-with in the world. The Other can be missing only *in* and *for* a Being-with (pp. 156–157).

Being-with-Others is presented as a dimension of being-in-the-world, which has the property of alienating Dasein from its own true self. This is because Dasein's concern for others supposedly includes a constant care as to the way one differs from them. Such care disturbs being-with-one-another and gives rise to a tendency to become like others, to allow them to define who and what one should be.

Dasein, as everyday Being-with-one-another, stands in *subjection* to Others. It itself *is* not; its Being has been taken away by the Others. Dasein's everyday possibilities of Being are for the others to dispose of as they please" (p. 164).
Being-with-one-another dissolves one's own Dasein completely into the kind of Being of "the Others" (p. 164).

The others to whom one's autonomy is surrendered are collectively known as "the they" (das Man). The responsibility of defending one's independent selfhood is a heavy burden according to Heidegger, and Dasein therefore turns to the anonomous social milieu for the guiding directives of life. "The they" to which Dasein turns brings forth the self of everydayness, the "they-self" (das Man-Selbst), which is sharply distinguished from the so-called "authentic self." Heidegger claims that the constancy of identity experienced in ordinary social life is a manifestation of the dictatorship of "the they," which creates an enduring they-self in collusion with Dasein's inauthenticity and failure to stand by its own deepest possibilities. The existential movement of becoming absorbed and lost in the publicness of "the they" is known as "falling" (Verfallen), and is described as the dominant state of being which belongs to man.

[Falling into inauthenticity] amounts to a quite distinctive kind of Being-in-the-world—the kind which is completely fascinated by the "world" and by the Dasein-with of Others in "the they." Not-being-its-self functions as a *positive* possibility of that entity which, in its essential concern, is absorbed in a world. This kind of not-Being has to be conceived as that kind of Being which is closest to Dasein and in which Dasein maintains itself for the most part (p. 220).

In falling, Dasein falls away from itself into a state of groundless floating. This state is a tranquilizing one, for fallenness into the world has the sanction of "the they" and gives the appearance of being a secure and genuine mode of existence. But this drifting along is actually a drifting toward self-alienation in which one's ownmost potentialities and concerns become hidden and lost.

Falling may also be characterized as a *fleeing*, where the flight is from Dasein's own authentic nature as being-in-the-world. Heidegger introduces the concept of *anxiety* at this point to refer to the state of mind underlying falling. Anxiety is the opposite of the tranquilization of "the they;" it is the existential mood that individualizes Dasein and frees it for the realization of its most essential possibilities. Closely related to anxiety is the "uncanniness" (Unheimlichkeit) of authentic being, a sense of not-being-at-home, which Heidegger claims accompanies Dasein's union with its own deepest self. Falling numbs Dasein to the uncanniness of authentic selfhood, replacing anxiety with the tranquilized familiarity of everydayness. At the same time this uncanniness of being, which is escaped through embracing the they-self, is existentially a more fundamental attribute of Dasein's constitution.

Heidegger continues his explication of the a priori structure of human existence by taking up the relationship between authenticity and death as possibilities of Dasein's being. Dasein is wholly itself, according to his analysis, only when there is nothing left outstanding for it to be, only at its end, in death. An intimate bond is said to connect the reality of death as an existentially constitutive element of Dasein with the possibility of Dasein achieving a full and deep-ranging authenticity. This is because death is the one thing in one's possession that cannot be taken away.

> No one can take the Other's dying away from him . . . . Dying is something that every Dasein itself must take upon itself at the time. By its very essence, death is in every case mine, in so far as it "is" at all (p. 294).

Heidegger's ontological descriptions show that he regards death as having the power to dissolve the they-self and liberate Dasein in its fullest authenticity.

> With death, Dasein stands before itself in its ownmost potentiality-for-Being . . . . If Dasein stands there before itself as this possibility, it has been *fully* assigned to its ownmost potentiality-for-Being. When it stands before itself in this way, all its relations to any other Dasein have been undone. This ownmost non-relational possibility is at the same time the uttermost one (p. 294).
> [In being-toward-death] it can become manifest to Dasein that in this distinctive possibility of its own self, it has been wrenched away from "the they" (p. 307).

Of course it is possible for death to be incorporated into the superficial talk of "the they," in which case the individual's anxiety at confronting the inevitability of coming to an end is replaced with tranquilizing formulae such as, "Death certainly comes, but not right away" (p. 302). Such a formula, embraced in falling, defers the reality of death and covers up what is central in an authentic view of death's certainty—"that it is possible at any moment" (p. 302). Heidegger stresses again and again that death, by virtue of being a property of Dasein that cannot be appropriated by other Daseins, enables one to individualize himself and stake a claim to his ownmost being. By passionately seizing upon the inevitability of death, Dasein secures the foundation for living its life in an authentic and autonomous way.

> When, by anticipation, one becomes free *for* one's own death, one is liberated from lostness in ["the they"] and one is liberated in such a way that *for the first time* one can authentically understand and choose among the factical possibilities lying ahead of that possiblity which is death (p. 308, italics added).

In the world of Heidegger's thought, the individual's relationship to his ownmost being or self is radically in question. In this context his litany of the existentialia may be viewed as an attempt by Dasein to move away from alienation and falling and toward a representation of its own individual selfhood. Specifically, by identifying the structural constituents of human existence and projecting these elements into the ontological foundation of man's being, Dasein seeks to replace a sense of groundless floating with a picture of its own deepest roots. It is difficult to escape the impression of a certain emptiness in the results of this effort; one learns much more about what Dasein is *not* rather than what it *is*. It sometimes even appears that the sole positive characteristic possessed by Dasein is its tendency to attribute to itself characteristics which in reality it does not possess. The very existence of *Being and Time,* however, points to the presence in Dasein's nature of a countervailing tendency to throw off the disguises of falling. Heidegger labels the primordial inclination of Dasein to restore itself to itself "the call of conscience." Conscience is said to issue a call that pushes "the they" into insignifi-

cance and summons the self to its ownmost possibility of being-
itself. This call comes forth from that same existential location
which Dasein in falling seeks to escape; namely, the uncanniness
of individualized being-in-the-world.

> Conscience manifests itself as the call of care: the caller is Dasein,
> which in its thrownness (in its Being-already-in) is anxious about
> its   potentiality-for-Being .... Dasein   is   falling   into   "the
> they" . . . and it is summoned out of this falling by the appeal (p.
> 322).

The task of assessing the significance of Heidegger's *Being and
Time* confronts the psychoanalytic theorist with a dilemma. This
work is in the first place an investigation in ontology, aiming at
clarifying the meaning of being as such. The question of the
meaning of being, as we understand it, does not enter the field of
concern of psychoanalysis, even at the level of pretheoretical assumptions. The analyst takes it for granted that man *is,* and further that the nature of man's being can be studied productively
without considering the problem of being in general. At the same
time psychoanalytic research is obviously not a philosophically
neutral activity. It is based on premises about its subject matter
and these premises guide and delimit the investigations it under-
takes. There are at least two general ways in which the philosophical commitments of psychoanalytic phenomenology resemble those of Heidegger's existential analytic of Dasein. First, both
inquiries begin with a conception of man as an experiencing being, situated in a world involving human purposes and meanings.
Second, the contemporary analyst recognizes that man's interpretation of himself in terms of categories applying to material objects in his world effectively prevents his understanding of himself *as man.* A divergence between Heidegger's analysis and the
psychoanalytic approach appears, however, when we come to consider the finer details of the ontological characterization of
Dasein. Heidegger singles out the tendency for man to mistak-
enly view himself in terms of that which he is not as the pivotal
fact of human nature. Human beings have, as one of their existential possibilities, the possibility of becoming depersonalized
and estranged from their own natures. Such an estrangement in-

deed is exemplified in the objectifying images of man's nature that have dominated the human sciences in the 20th Century. But to locate this alienation in man's ontological constitution makes it something that must be presupposed by every inquiry into human life. Such a postulate unnaturally magnifies the significance of this one human possibility to the exclusion of all others, and confers upon the resulting vision of mankind a very specific limiting focus. From a psychoanalytic vantage point, the polarity between authentic and inauthentic modes of being defines a dimension of human self-experience. It is not the problem of being as such that interests the analyst, but rather the problem of understanding the varied forms of the *individual experience of being*. The elucidation of this experience takes place on an empirical plane, in studies of specific personal worlds and their development.

Heidegger's *Being and Time* cries out to be read from a psychobiographical as well as a philosophical perspective. Such a reading unveils the contribution of this work as a fascinating descriptive study of human self-estrangement. The ontology of Dasein may then be understood as a *symbol* of an anguished struggle for individuality and grounded authenticity in a world where one is in perpetual danger of absorption in the pressures and influences of the social milieu.

Jean-Paul Sartre

A phenomenological system bearing a resemblance to that of Heidegger appears in the philosophy of Jean-Paul Sartre. This system, which presents an ontology of consciousness, is developed most fully in the central work, *Being and Nothingness* (1943).[4] The nature of consciousness, according to Sartre, is radically different from the nature of objects. Consciousness is a mode of being which exists for itself, whereas an object exists only in itself. The world of human existence is thus divided into two distinct and non-overlapping regions: *being-for-itself* and *being-in-itself.* Being-for-itself is characterized by Sartre as composed of pure

[4]All references in the section on Sartre, unless otherwise indicated, are from this book.

non-being or nothingness. This is in contrast to being-in-itself, which is understood as a fullness or plenitude of being. No description of the for-itself is possible within the Sartrean framework except in terms of that which it is not, namely in-itself. The nothingness that constitutes the nature of consciousness is a matter of literal negativity and insufficiency, subsisting in the midst of the fullness of the world of things. Moreover, it is inherent in consciousness to be aware of its nature as incompleteness and nothingness.

> Consciousness is a being, the nature of which is to be conscious of the nothingness of its being (p. 86).
> The pure event by which human reality rises as a presence in the world is apprehended by itself as its own lack. In its coming into existence human reality grasps itself as an incomplete being (p. 139).

What is missing in the for-itself is a substantial foundation which would give it the positive characteristics of self-identity and permanence possessed by objects in the world of the in-itself.

Sartre writes that being-in-itself simply "is what it is," whereas being-for-itself "is what it is not and is not what it is." This formula is meant to emphasize that consciousness does not coincide with itself in the same manner that an object does. Whatever particular role or identity is assumed by a person, this identity is never identical to the person who has assumed it. For example, if a man is a cafe waiter, he is not a waiter in the same way a table is a table. He is being a waiter "in the mode of not being one." Human consciousness does not possess any features that would give it self-identity. "What the for-itself lacks is the self—or itself as in-itself . . . . The missing in-itself is pure absence" (p. 138). Not only does Sartre's philosophy make a sharp distinction between the for-itself and the in-itself, it protrays the for-itself as itself engaged in this same sharply differentiating activity.

> The for-itself is perpetually determining itself not to be the in-itself. This means that it can establish itself only in terms of the in-itself and against the in-itself (p. 134).

The concept of consciousness as a species of non-being is intimately tied to the Sartrean doctrine of man's *freedom*. Consciousness is regarded as a perpetual spontaneity, radically free in the sense that it determines itself at every instant and is never determined by anything external to itself. The objects comprising the realm of being-in-itself are subject to external causation, whereas consciousness is *no-thing;* it has no permanent features, no substantiality, and no causal dependence on things. It is in this context that one may understand the famous existentialist formula: "Existence precedes essence." If the for-itself had an essence or pre-existing nature defining it and remaining constant throughout its vicissitudes, it would thereby join the world of things and become subject to the laws that govern the world of things. But it has no determinate nature or essence except the one it freely chooses, and each of its choices is vulnerable to overthrow and transformation from one moment to the next. Man is thus separated from himself as he was and as he will be; stability and continuity through time are properties not of consciousness but of objects.

Sartre's emphasis on the radical freedom of consciousness is an expression of his more general tendency always to stress the differences between the for-itself and the in-itself. This differentiating, separating trend, however, is actually just one side of a dialectical struggle in which the for-itself is engaged; for man's recognition of his nothingness and his freedom does not lie peacefully upon him. A clear awareness of freedom means an acknowledgement that one is the absolute creator of himself and his destiny. The extraordinary responsibility implied by this role is felt as *anguish,* and a longing arises in consciousness to escape from freedom into the secure solidity and self-identity possessed by things in the world of the in-itself.

> freedom, which manifests itself through anguish, is characterized by a constantly renewed obligation to remake the *self* which designates the free being (p. 73).
> We flee from anguish by attempting to apprehend ourselves . . . as *a thing* (p. 82).
> Everything takes place . . . as if our essential and immediate behavior with respect to anguish is flight . . . to fill the void which encircles us, to re-establish the links between past and present, be-

tween present and future . . . [We thereby seek] the absolute
positivity of being-in-itself (p. 78–79).

The flight from anguish through embracing the illusion of being thing-like Sartre calls *bad faith*. In the attitude of bad faith,
the heavy burden of human freedom is lifted as man pretends to
possess a determinate nature which he can hold responsible for
who he is. The problem with the attempt to appropriate to the for-
itself the positive attributes of the in-itself is that were this project to succeed, the for-itself would be extinguished. An individual
can genuinely escape freedom—the ever-renewed responsibility
for defining who he is—only in death. Consciousness is, therefore,
trapped in an irresolvable contradiction: It is an insufficiency
seeking to complete itself by adopting the permanence and substantiality of things, but its efforts in this direction are blocked by
the grim fact that being permanent and substantial would also
mean becoming inert and dead.

> The being of human reality is suffering because it [can] not attain
> the in-itself without losing the for-itself. Human reality is there-
> fore by nature an unhappy consciousness with no possibility of sur-
> passing its unhappy state (p. 140).

Being-for-itself moves in two directions with respect to the in-
itself. It differentiates itself from things by affirming its freedom
and acknowledging its nothingness, and it attempts to identify itself with things by fleeing from anguish and engaging in acts of
bad faith. This to-and-fro movement between being and non-
being lends a tragic dimension to human existence. Its goal is to
achieve a state which actually is impossible, namely a transcend-
ent fusion of the spontaneity of consciousness with the substantiality and permanence of objects.

> [This state would be] the impossible synthesis of the for-itself and
> in-itself; it would be its own foundation not as nothingness but as
> being and would preserve within it the necessary translucency of
> consciousness along with the coincidence with itself [self-identity]
> of being-in-itself (p. 134).

It is our impression that Sartre's writings contain a hidden attempt to achieve the "impossible synthesis" of being-for-itself and

being-in-itself. This attempt appears in the reification of the concept of nothingness, i.e., the transformation of the absence of the attributes of a thing into a literal gap or insufficiency in the universe, a hole in the fabric of the world presented as man's true nature. The conception of the for-itself as an *actual lack of being* places consciousness on the same factual plane of reality occupied by the tangible substances of the in-itself. The doctrine of the radical freedom of the subject may be interpreted as an elaboration of this conflict-reducing reification. In a striking contradication of his thesis that man has no essence which precedes his existence, Sartre posits freedom as the *essential* feature of human consciousness. By visualizing man's nothingness as freedom, he changes a supposed lack of definition and temporal continuity into a permanent positive characteristic of human nature. This change has the added effect of conferring upon consciousness an enduring self-identity.

A third category of being is also extensively described by Sartre, and is of utmost significance in understanding and evaluating his conception of the human situation. This is the category of *being-for-others*. The for-itself, in its apprehension of other persons, regards them as objects in its experiential field. The subjective consciousness belonging to an individual can never be directly known except by that individual himself; what it is *for itself* is radically different from what it is *for others*. In addition, consciousness cannot directly know the self which it is for-the-Other, because this self comes into being only as the object of the Other's awareness.

> I am incapable of apprehending for myself the self which I am for the Other, just as I am incapable of apprehending on the basis of the *Other-as-object* which appears to me, what the Other is for himself (p. 327).

The consequences of the "objectness" of being-for-others include a severe threat to the continued life of the for-itself as an autonomous center of freedom. When a person comes under the gaze of another, he grasps the Other as a freedom that constitutes a world of meanings and possibilities around itself. This understanding may then extend to a sudden recognition that he is himself in the process of being articulated within the structures of that alien world, which threatens to displace his own and absorb him into pure objectness. He senses a foreign outline being imposed upon his nothingness, and without knowing what this outline is he feels himself being stripped of his subjectivity and transformed into an object. ". . . once more the in-itself closes in upon the for-itself . . . . I have an outside, I have a *nature*" (p. 352). When one is made the object of the Other's look, an "internal haemorrhage" occurs in one's subjective world, which then flows in the direction of the Other's freedom. Sartre describes this relationship of one consciousness to another as analogous to slavery.

> I am a slave [to the Other] to the degree that my being is dependent at the center of a freedom which is not mine and which is the very condition of my being . . . insofar as I am the instrument of possibilities which are not my possibilities, whose pure presence beyond my being I cannot even glimpse, and which deny my transcendence in order to constitute me as a means to ends of which I am ignorant—*I am in danger*. This danger is not an accident but the permanent structure of my being-for-others (p. 358).

It is worth remarking that Sartre finds in this endangerment of being-for-itself a "permanent structure," i.e., a tenuous yet enduring way in which personal consciousness achieves its longed-for state of self-identity.

The response of being-for-itself to the threat of reduction to the status of an object in being-for-others is to deny the freedom of the other by reducing *him* to an object.

> The objectivation of the Other . . . is a defense on the part of my being which, precisely by conferring on the Other a being-for-me, frees me from my being-for-the-Other (p. 359).

The loss of freedom and the imprisonment of subjectivity in being-for-others is vividly symbolized by the image of damnation in Sartre's play *No Exit* (1946). Here the principal characters are condemned for eternity to know themselves only through the frozen images they have of one another's odious lives. Human relationships are thus pictured as never-ending battles between competing subjectivities struggling to strip each other of freedom and reduce each other to objects.

In the theoretical world of Jean-Paul Sartre, the subjective being of the individual is perpetually threatened by the objectivating, engulfing power of alien consciousness.[5] This image of interpersonal life is one in which the person is constantly being absorbed into roles with which he cannot truly identify. Sartre's treatment of social relationships does not include the possibility of being empathically understood in such a manner that one's sense of self is mirrored and enhanced rather than ensnared and degraded. This omission is of great significance, for once the experience of such empathy is introduced into the structure of being-for-others, the tensions and conflicts which plague the for-itself undergo a complete transformation. Social life ceases to be a battleground of competing subjectivities locked in a life-and-death struggle to annihilate one another. The relationship to the other becomes instead a realm of experience in which one's personal selfhood can rest secure, indeed, in which it can be powerfully affirmed.

Psychoanalytic methods and ideas could never arise on the basis of Sartre's ontology of consciousness. This is because psychoanalysis is a science of the intersubjective, grounded in empathic dialogue between two persons. The analyst presupposes that he *can* apprehend what he is for-his-patient, and also what his patient is for-himself; it is further assumed that this understanding can develop in a collaborative endeavor posing no intrinsic threat to the self-definitions of the persons involved. In a psychotherapeutic relationship patterned consistently on the principles of *Being and Nothingness,* by contrast, the analyst could encounter his patient only as the carrier of an alien and hostile world, a dangerous enemy to be neutralized through reduction to the status of an object.

We would also take exception to the notion of freedom developed in Sartre's philosophy. The problem with this idea is that it

---

[5]Deep insight into the personal background of this image of interpersonal life can be gained from a reading of Sartre's autobiographical fragment, *The Words* (1964). For a study of the relationship between the themes of this autobiography and his philosophy, see Atwood (1983).

elevates a specific attribute of self-experience to an ontological level of man's being, making it something that must be assumed to be present at the heart of every person's world. The doctrine of the radical freedom of the subject renders Sartre's framework incapable of adequately describing and accounting for human situations in which this experience is not the central one. Moreover, by locating spontaneity and autonomy in the very essence of consciousness, his thought deters the pursuit of questions about the developmental origins and vicissitudes of the experience of personal freedom. The study of such questions is an important part of the psychoanalytic quest for understanding of the genesis of human selfhood.

Sartre's writings nevertheless contain a significant contribution to psychoanalytic knowledge. The philosopher Charles Hanly (1979) hints at the nature of this contribution with his interesting suggestion that Sartre's theory of consciousness applies more clearly to the psychological disorder known as "as-if personality" than to human subjectivity in general. *Being and Nothingness* may be read as a richly elaborated phenomenology of those subjective states in which a lack of full consolidation of the structure of self-experience results in the problem of self-definition becoming the person's central preoccupation.

Conclusion

Each of the three phenomenological systems reviewed above is a proposal concerning the assumptions underlying the study of human experience. These proposals have in common an emphasis on differentiating between the properties of material objects in the world of experience and the properties of subjectivity itself. This same emphasis has been of growing importance in recent psychoanalytic thought, specifically in the critique of Freudian metapsychology. It seems to us that this agreement establishes the possibility of an integration of phenomenological insight into psychoanalysis. In the past there have been two main obstacles to such integration. The first of these was the commitment of analysts to a vision of their field modeled on the image of the natural sciences. This commitment is enshrined in the metaphorical language of classical metapsychology, which pictures mental life in terms of forces, energies, mechanisms, and a reign of causal determinism. The second obstacle was an insufficiently critical attitude toward the phenomenological philosophers themselves. Many exceptional thinkers have tried to restructure the assumptions of psychoanalysis along existential-phenomenological lines (e.g., Binswanger, 1963; Boss, 1963; 1979; May, Angel, & Ellenberger, 1958). We are in sympathy with such reformulations, insofar as their aim has been to free the phenomenological knowledge of psychoanalysis from its procrustean bed of mechanism and determinism. What has limited the success of so-called "existential analysis," however, has been its tendency uncritically to import into psychoanalytic theory philosophical concepts and categories not genuinely grounded in clinical observation. To introduce Heidegger's ontology of Dasein in place of Freud's assumptions about human nature, for example, appears to us of questionable value in advancing psychoanalytic knowledge as a whole. A truly *psychoanalytic* phenomenology resists the philosopher's temptation to define consciousness in universal terms and instead seeks understanding of the phenomena transpiring in the specific intersubjective dialogue of the psychoanalytic situation.

STRUCTURALISM

The third tradition of thought upon which psychoanalytic phenomenology draws is that of modern structuralism. Structuralism is an intellectual movement cutting across a wide variety of disciplines, including psychology, philosophy, cultural anthropology, linguistics, and literary criticism. In what follows, we shall not discuss specific conceptual systems in these varied fields that are designated "structuralist;" our focus will instead be on certain general features such inquiry exhibits and on how it is that these features are also characteristic of psychoanalysis.

At its most abstract level, the notion of a structural analysis refers to a method for reaching a particular mode of understanding. The use of this method implies first of all an interest in the relations *among* the specific phenomena being explored rather

than in any of those phenomena taken in isolation. The empirical
domain of structural investigation is assumed to be intelligible in
terms of ordering principles or patterns. These principles are *im-
manent*, in the sense of belonging intrinsically to the phenomena
being analyzed, so that a structural analysis deals exclusively
with intrinsic relations and does not seek to explain its subject
matter on the basis of extraneous factors.

Structural analysis may be contrasted with causal analysis. A
causal investigation is concerned with what has immediately preceded the phenomena under study and conceives of events as a
linear unfolding in time. The aim of a causal analysis is to
achieve a comprehensive explanation, meaning an exhaustive
specification of the determining influences prevailing in a situation. To those who are guided by this aim, a structuralist inquiry
would probably appear to be a merely descriptive enterprise. The
reason for this is that structural thought is not concerned with
isolating cause-effect connections, but rather seeks understanding of the interrelations linking different phenomena into structural unities or wholes. The concept of a structural whole is an
abstract idea referring to the context of relationships in which an
event is embedded. Although one sometimes speaks of phenomena being "generated" or "organized" by structures, or of structures being "actualized" by events, these processes are not interpreted as linear causal sequences occurring in time. Structures
have no existence apart from the phenomena in which they are
discerned. A structural analysis is nevertheless *not* a merely descriptive account; on the contrary, it unveils a coherence and sim-
plicity within phenomena, which are not visible at the level of
description.

The central role assigned to the axis of time by causal thinking
leads to the use of *prediction* as a criterion for assessing the adequacy of an explanation. This is because a comprehensive causal
account of a system of events allows in principle a forecasting of
that system's future. The empirical field of a structuralist inquiry, on the other hand, does not possess the features of a closed
causal system and may indeed be open and thus inherently
unpredictable. To be unpredictable at the level of concrete events

does not however mean being unlawful at the level of the patterning of those events. The adequacy of a structural explanation is measured not by its predictive power, but rather by the degree to which it brings together in one unitary interpretation domains that, at first sight, seem disconnected to the observer. A key concept in this integrating function is that of *invariance*. Invariance refers here to a structural configuration that remains constant over some set of transformations. The aim of a structural analysis is to reduce the initial apparent disarray in a system of observed facts by illuminating the invariant structural configurations organizing that system.

This characterization of structuralism applies to psychoanalytic thought extremely well. Psychoanalysis is and always has been a science of the structure of subjectivity, concerned with the patterns organizing personal experience and conduct. Although its early formulations were colored by a determinism adopted from the natural sciences of the 19th Century, its real contribution was in the placing of various psychological phenomena in the structural contexts of meaning to which they belonged. It is our belief that the language of structuralism is uniquely appropriate for the expresion of psychoanalytic knowledge, and this book as a whole represents an effort to rethink psychoanalysis from a structuralist point of view. We complete this chapter by giving brief discussions of traditionally central psychoanalytic concepts in the structuralist language of psychoanalytic phenomenology. These discussions at the same time serve to introduce the clinical and theoretical issues taken up in greater detail in later chapters.

Personality Structure

From the perspective of psychoanalytic phenomenology, personality structure is the *structure of a person's experiencing*. Thus, the basic units of analysis for our investigations of personality are *structures of experience*—the distinctive configurations of self and object that shape and organize a person's subjective world. These psychological structures are not to be viewed simply as "internalizations" or mental replicas of interpersonal events. Nor

should they be regarded as having an objective existence in physical space or somewhere in a "mental apparatus." Instead, we
conceptualize these structures as systems of ordering or
organizing principles (Piaget, 1970b)—cognitive-affective sche-
mata (Klein, 1976; Slap & Saykin, 1980) through which a person's experiences of self and other assume their characteristic
forms and meanings. Such structures of subjectivity are disclosed
in the thematic patterning of a person's subjective life.

In psychoanalytic phenomenology the concept of *character* is
coextensive with the structure of a subjective world. This conception of character rests on the assumption of a close functional relationship between the structuralization of human experience
and the patterning of human conduct. Specifically, we assume
that recurrent patterns of conduct serve to actualize (Sandler &
Sandler, 1978) the nuclear configurations of self and object that
constitute a person's character. This functional relationship is explored in chapter 4.

While "personality" and "character" are extremely broad concepts pertaining to the overall structure of a subjective universe,
self is a more delimited and specific term referring to the structure of a person's experience of himself. The self, from the vantage point of psychoanalytic phenomenology, is a psychological
structure through which self-experience acquires cohesion and
continuity, and by virtue of which self-experience assumes its
characteristic shape and enduring organization. We have found it
important to distinguish sharply between the concept of the self
as a psychological structure and the concept of the *person* as an
experiencing subject and agent who initiates action. Whereas the
self-as-structure falls squarely within the domain of psychoanalytic investigation, the ontology of the person-as-agent, in our
view, lies beyond the scope of psychoanalytic inquiry. Psychoanalysis can only illuminate the *experience* of personal agency or
its absence in specific contexts of meaning.

The concept of the self as psychological structure clarifies
Heinz Kohut's unique contributions to psychoanalytic thought.
His central contributions to our understanding of psychopathology, for example, concern those states in which the psychological
structure that organizes the experience of self is missing or unsteady (Kohut, 1971, 1977).

Motivation

Psychoanalytic phenomenology does not postulate a theory of the nature of personality as an "objective entity." Instead, it consists in a methodological system of interpretive principles to guide the study of meaning in human experience and conduct. Its explanatory concepts thus emphasize not "psychic determinism" and a natural science view of casuality, but rather a *subjective contextualism* that brings to focus the nexus of personal meanings in which a person's experience and conduct are embedded. Rather than formulating impersonal motivational prime movers of a mental apparatus, psychoanalytic phenomenology seeks to illuminate the multiple conscious and unconscious purposes (Klein, 1976) or personal reasons (Schafer, 1976) that lead a person to strive to actualize his psychological structures.

The evolution of our framework has led us to propose an additional, more general, supraordinate motivational principle: that the *need to maintain the organization of experience* is a central motive in the patterning of human action. The significance of this motivational principle and the light it sheds on the fundamental role played by concrete symbolization in human psychological life provide the focus of chapter 4.

Repression and the Unconscious

In psychoanalytic phenomenology, repression is understood as a process whereby particular configurations of self and object are prevented from crystallizing in awareness. Repression may thus be viewed as a *negative organizing principle* operating alongside the positive organizing principles underlying the configurations that do repeatedly materialize in conscious experience. The "dynamic unconscious," from this point of view, consists in that set of configurations that consciousness is not permitted to assume, because of their association with emotional conflict and subjective danger. Particular memories, fantasies, feelings, and other experiential contents are repressed because they threaten to actualize these configurations. Other defenses are conceptualized as further transformations of the subjective world that prevent dreaded configurations from emerging by radically altering and restricting the person's experience of self and other (Stolorow & Atwood, 1979).

In addition to the "dynamic unconscious," viewed as a system of negative organizing principles, another form of unconsciousness has increasingly assumed a position of importance in our framework. The organizing principles of a person's subjective world, whether operating positively (giving rise to certain configurations in awareness), or negatively (preventing certain configurations from arising), are themselves unconscious. A person's experiences are shaped by his psychological structures without this shaping becoming the focus of awareness and reflection. We have therefore characterized the structure of a subjective world as *prereflectively unconscious.*[6] This form of unconsciousness is not the product of defensive activity, even though great effort is required to overcome it. In fact, the defenses themselves, when operating outside a person's awareness, can be seen as merely a special instance of structuring activity that is prereflectively unconscious.

In the absence of reflection, a person is unaware of his role as a constitutive subject in elaborating his personal reality. The world in which he lives and moves presents itself as though it were something independently and objectively real. The patterning and thematizing of events that uniquely characterize his personal reality are thus seen as if they were properties of those events rather than products of his own subjective interpretations and constructions. As we indicate in chapter 2, psychoanalytic therapy can be viewed as a procedure through which a patient acquires reflective knowledge of this unconscious structuring activity.

Personality Development

In psychoanalytic phenomenology, personality development refers to the *structuralization of personal experience.* Efforts to construct a psychoanalytic developmental psychology of the subjec-

---

[6]The concept of the prereflective unconscious has features in common with Levi-Strauss's (1963) and Piaget's (1972) postulations of unconscious structures of thought that are not repressed, and with Lacan's (1958) idea that the unconscious is structured like a language.

tive world are still in their infancy. They have been significantly hampered, we feel, by the persistent psychological tradition of artificially dividing human subjectivity into cognitive and affective domains—a fragmentation of psychic reality that has tended to preclude an integration of psychoanalytic knowledge with the wealth of research findings on the perceptual and cognitive development of children. A psychoanalytic developmental psychology concerned with the structuralization of experience would be especially enriched by articulations with the developmental-structural psychology of Piaget (see Basch, 1977, and Greenspan, 1979). With a mending of the rift between cognition and affect, and a focusing on the ontogenesis of unitary configurations of (cognitive-affective) experience, Piagetian concepts such as the principles of structural assimilation and accommodation become especially germane for conceptualizing the course of personality development.

Two ubiquitous psychological processes—differentiation and integration—play a pivotal role in the evolution of the subjective world. A brief description of these developmental processes as they have been presumed to operate in early childhood will serve to illustrate our conception of personality development as the structuralization of experience (see Stolorow & Atwood, 1979, and Stolorow & Lachmann, 1980). In chapter 3 we examine the specific intersubjective contexts in which these and other developmental processes are facilitated or obstructed.

It has been generally assumed that in the earliest phase of infancy self and object are not consistently differentiated. Gradually, the neonate acquires the capacity to discriminate reliably between his own sensations and the objects from which they are derived (Jacobson, 1964). Thus, perhaps the first developmental task to face the infant, central to the beginning structuralization of his subjective world, is the subjective differentiation of self from primary objects—the rudimentary establishment of self-object boundaries (Mahler, Pine, & Bergman, 1975). The small child's incomplete attainment of self-object boundaries makes it both necessary and possible for him to rely on parental figures as "selfobjects" whose idealized attributes and mirror functions provide him with the self-cohesion and self-continuity that he cannot yet maintain on his own (Kohut, 1971, 1977). The child's growing capacity for self-object differentiation develops in concert with the emergence of symbolization and the ability to distinguish his own symbolizing activity from the objects being symbolized—important milestones in the evolution of his subjectivity.

Another characteristic of the very young infant's world is his inability to integrate experiences with contrasting affective colorations. Thus, a second developmental task, coincident with that of self-object differentiation, is the synthesis of object experiences colored with positive affect and object experiences colored with negative affect into an integrated perception of a whole object with both positive and negative qualities, coupled with a similar synthesis of affectively contrasting self-experiences into an integrated perception of the whole self (Kernberg, 1976).

From the standpoint of the object world, the attainment of differentiation and integration is reflected in the achievement of "object constancy"—the capacity to sustain an enduring image of another person who is valued for his positive and negative qualities and is recognized as a separate individual with needs and feelings of his own. From the standpoint of the self, the attainment of differentiation and integration is reflected in the establishment of a cohesive image of the self that is temporally stable and has an affective coloration more or less independent of immediate environmental support. Such "self constancy" has been described in terms of the subjective sense of identity (Erikson, 1956) and the continuity of self-esteem (Jacobson, 1964; Kohut, 1971, 1977, Lichtenberg, 1975).

The particular thematic structure of the child's subjective world will evolve organically from the critical formative experiences that mark his unique early history and the individualized array of personal motivations that develops as their result. Once the child has established a relatively constant and stable psychological organization, it will serve as a prereflective frame of reference into whose structure he will unconsciously assimilate his subsequent experiences. Developmental change will occur when this structure is altered and expanded to accommodate new constellations of experience.

From this phenomenological and developmental-structural perspective, Kohut's (1971, 1977) central contribution to our knowledge of personality development has been his conceptualization of the structuralization of self-experience. Two concepts pivotal to his formulation of the evolution of self-structure are "selfobject" and "transmuting internalization." A selfobject may be described phenomenologically as an object that a person experiences as incompletely separated from himself and that serves to maintain his sense of self. Transmuting internalization, described phenomenologically, is an enduring re-organization of the subjective field in which experienced qualities of a selfobject are translocated and assimilated into the child's own self-structure. These two developmental concepts—selfobject and transmuting internalization—are singularly important contributions to a psychoanalytic developmental psychology emphasizing the structuralization of experience.

An aspect of personality development that has been of particular interest to analysts is the role of psychosexual symbols in the evolution of the subjective world. This we take up in chapter 4.

Psychological Health and Pathology

A theory of personality development centering on the structuralization of experience will seek a conception of psychological health in some formulation of *optimal structuralization.* This ideal can be conceptualized in terms of the healthy person's ability to achieve an optimal balance between the maintenance of his psychological organization on the one hand and his openness to new forms of experience on the other. On the one hand, his psychological structures have become sufficiently consolidated so that they can assimilate a wide range of experiences of self and other and still retain their integrity and stability. His subjective world, in other words, is not unduly vulnerable to disintegration or dissolution. On the other hand, his psychological structures are sufficiently flexible to accommodate new configurations of experience of self and other, so that the organization of his subjective life can continue to expand in both complexity and scope.

Correspondingly, we can conceptualize two broad classes of psychopathology reflecting the two types of failure to attain this optimal balance. On the one hand, there are psychological disorders that reflect the consolidation of *pathological structures* that operate rigidly to restrict the person's subjective field. Examples are found in those persons whose lives are severely constricted by defensive structures that inflexibly order their experiences to prevent the emergence of emotional conflict and subjective danger. On the other hand, there are psychological disturbances that reflect *insufficient or faulty structuralization*—developmental deficiencies and arrests in the formation and consolidation of the subjective world (Stolorow & Lachmann, 1980). Examples are found in the persons described by Kohut (1971, 1977) who are prone to self-fragmentation and require immersion in archaic ties to selfobjects to sustain the cohesion and continuity of their precarious self-experiences. As we demonstrate in the next chapter, this distinction between pathological structure and insufficient structuralization holds important implications for conceptualizing the differing modes of therapeutic action of psychoanalytic treatment. We turn now to an examination of the intersubjective context in which the psychoanalytic process unfolds.

2   INTERSUBJECTIVITY: I. THE THERAPEUTIC SITUATION[1]

A science is defined by its domain of inquiry. In its most general form, our thesis in this chapter is that psychoanalysis seeks to illuminate phenomena that emerge within a specific psychological field constituted by the intersection of two subjectivities—that of the patient and that of the analyst. In this conceptualization, psychoanalysis is not seen as a science of the intrapsychic, focused on events presumed to occur within one isolated "mental apparatus." Nor is it conceived as a social science, investigating the "behavioral facts" of the therapeutic interaction as seen from a point of observation outside the field under study. Rather, psychoanalysis is pictured here as a science of the *intersubjective,* focused on the interplay between the differently organized subjective worlds of the observer and the observed. The observational stance is always one within, rather than outside, the intersubjective field or "contextual unit" (Schwaber, 1979) being observed, a fact that guarantees the centrality of introspection and empathy as the methods of observation (Kohut, 1959). Psychoanalysis is unique

[1]The development of this chapter benefited greatly from discussions with Dr. Bernard Brandchaft, who coauthored an earlier work on this subject (Stolorow, Brandchaft, & Atwood, 1983).

among the sciences in that the observer is also the observed (Stolorow & Atwood, 1979). In this chapter we examine the implications of this curious intersubjective situation for four issues that are of critical concern in psychoanalytic treatment: the nature of transference and countertransference, the explanation of "negative therapeutic reactions," the psychoanalytic understanding of psychopathology, and the conceptualization of the therapeutic action of psychoanalysis. First, however, we offer some reflections on the nature of the psychoanalytic situation.

THE PSYCHOANALYTIC SITUATION

In chapter 1 we argued that in psychoanalysis the concept of character refers to the overall organization of a subjective universe and that such structures constitute a unique realm of unconsciousness that we have termed "prereflective." Now we add that as psychoanalytic treatment has evolved from symptom analysis to character analysis, the time-honored aim of making the unconscious conscious has increasingly come to apply to the organizing principles and dominant leitmotivs that prereflectively shape a patient's experiences and conduct. As the patient begins to acquire reflective knowledge of the thematic patterning of his psychological life, he becomes able to step back from what heretofore had seemed to be the sheer factuality of existence and hence to recognize his world as partially constituted by the structures of his own subjectivity.

The psychoanalytic situation and the technical precepts that govern it may be viewed as a set of facilitating conditions that permit the structure of a patient's subjective world to unfold maximally and find illumination in relatively pure culture in the analytic transference. Let us consider, in this regard, the significance of the "fundamental rule" of free-association, the so-called "rule of abstinence," and certain rules of interpretation, with an eye toward extracting the more general psychological and therapeutic principles that they exemplify.

What are the consequences of the fundamental rule for a patient's subjective experiences in the analytic situation? To the degree that his "stream of consciousness" is increasingly freed from the conventions of logical coherence and social propriety and from the more personal restrictions imposed by considerations of pride and moral self-evaluation, the recurrent configurations of self and object that unconsciously thematize his subjective experiences emerge in progressively bolder relief. Hence the fundamental rule partakes of the more general psychological principle that the structure of a person's subjective world is most readily discernible in his relatively unfettered, spontaneous productions—a principle that bears upon the particular psychoanalytic utility of dreams, fantasies, reverie states, whimsical and "incidental" thoughts, slips of the tongue, etc.

Resistance to free-association may be understood, in part, in terms of the patient's need to exclude from conscious experience those configurations of self and object that are associated with emotional conflict and subjective danger. In addition, it is essential to examine the ways in which the free-association process itself is assimilated by the structures of the patient's subjectivity. It is well known that for many patients free-association takes on a Janus-faced quality, in both offering a tempting relaxation of moral self-scrutiny and posing the threat of confronting dangerous inner promptings. Furthermore, the experience of free-associating may become colored by the imagery of any of the psychosexual modes. One patient experienced free-associating as a feeding of the analyst, with the promise of a reciprocal feasting in return, so that silences were feared as isolating periods of potentially endless emotional starvation. Another patient resisted free-association as both a relinquishment of precious psychic contents and a failure to contain destructive urges. Still another felt that to associate freely was to sexually titillate the analyst and to invite hurtful penetration, unconsciously assimilating the process to a dreaded oedipal configuration and primal scene image.

It is particularly essential to determine how free-association is experienced by patients whose subjective worlds are precariously structured in consequence of severe developmental interferences and arrests. One such patient filled her sessions with unceasing, carefully rehearsed talk about predetermined topics for fear that if the analyst were permitted to think any unforeseen thoughts about her, her fragile sense of self would be destroyed and she would become subject to unendurable feelings of nothingness. Another patient could tolerate neither free-associating nor silences because the structurelessness of each posed the threat of frightening merger experiences entailing loss of the capacity for self-object differentiation.

To summarize, not only does the fundamental rule enhance the unveiling of the patient's subjective world by encouraging him to permit the analytic material to unfold as a more or less spontaneous psychological product. In addition, the experience of free-associating is itself woven into the fabric of this world and becomes subject to its organizing principles and structural properties.

Freud (1919) enjoined that "analytic treatment should be carried through, as far as is possible, under privation—in a state of abstinence," meaning that the analyst must not offer his patients any instinctual satisfactions. Closely allied to this concept of abstinence is the recommended attitude of noninterfering neutrality and unobtrusive anonymity, by virtue of which the analyst was presumed to function as a kind of tabula rasa, a mirror reflecting back images from the patient's unconscious infantile history.

While these technical precepts are often justified by means of metapsychological constructions involving presumed vicissitudes of instinctual energies, we think they are best understood in terms of their impact upon the patient's subjective experience of the analytic relationship. Specifically, the noninterfering neutrality of the therapist can facilitate his ready assimilation into the psychological configurations that dominate the patient's subjective life. That these properties of the analytic situation promote the development of transference is an example of the general psychological principle that when an object is ambiguous its image is more clearly shaped and colored by the organizing principles of a person's own subjective world. This is not to say that a therapist who adopts a more interactive, personally revealing approach will not also become assimilated by the patient's psychological structures. Such assimilation is inevitable regardless of the therapist's behavior. However, the analytic attitude of neutrality can enhance the ease with which the patient's own psychological structures are discernible and demonstrable to the patient as recurrent forms and modalities that dominate his experience of the therapeutic relationship.

Careful attention to the patient's subjective frame of reference also reveals the ways in which the analyst's presumed neutrality may be sharply limited and circumscribed. The patient's experience of the therapist's acceptance and understanding of him may revive elements of the early mother-child dyad (Loewald, 1960), such that the analytic relationship functions as a "holding environment" (Winnicott, 1965; Modell, 1976) or archaic selfobject (Kohut, 1971, 1977), silently promoting psychological differentiation and integration. Especially in the treatment of severe developmental arrests, care must be taken that the principle of abstinence not include the patient's revived developmental needs, as when he might require resumption in the transference of a prematurely interrupted merger or acknowledgment of a developmental step toward greater separation (Stolorow & Lachmann, 1980). In such cases, excessively depriving "neutrality" on the part of the analyst in the name of technical purity might actually constitute an "error in humanity" (Stone, 1961; Greenson, 1967) that in its impact repeats the childhood traumata implicated in the genesis of the patient's psychopathology (Balint, 1969; Kohut, 1971; Stolorow & Lachmann, 1980).

We suggest that the rules of abstinence, neutrality, and anonymity can be subordinated to a more general and inclusive therapeutic principle that the analyst's actions in the therapeutic situation should as much as possible be determined by his understanding of the nature, origins, and functions of the configurations currently structuring the patient's subjective experiences. As a corollary, it follows that the analyst must continually scrutinize the ways in which all of the technical procedures and paraphernalia of the analytic situation (free-association, neutrality, use of the couch, frequency of sessions, payment of fees, etc.) become assimilated by and subject to the organizing principles of the patient's subjective world.

Let us now turn to a consideration of some of the technical rules of psychoanalytic interpretation, such as "interpretation always starts at the surface," "ego analysis precedes id analysis," and "interpretation of resistance precedes interpretation of content" (Fenichel, 1941). Analogously to the concept of abstinence, these rules have often been justified by metapsychological conceptions of the topographical layering of the "mental apparatus." How might such rules of interpretation be understood with reference to the unfolding of a subjective world?

In our view, the essential work of interpretation is to elucidate the nature, developmental origins, and functional significance of the psychological structures that prereflectively organize the patient's subjective experiences in general and thematize the transference relationship in particular. With regard to functional significance, we have seen that such recurrent configurations of self and object may serve a variety of conscious and unconscious purposes (wish-fulfilling, self-guiding and self-punishing, adaptive, restitutive-reparative, and defensive purposes) as they undergo various developmental vicissitudes in the course of a person's life cycle. While conceptually distinguishable, these functions are generally found to co-occur clinically, combined and amalgamated with one another in highly complex ways. Any significant configuration will have multiple origins and serve multiple purposes (Waelder, 1936). The rules of interpretation cited earlier can be subsumed under a more embracing therapeutic principle that interpretation should always be guided by an assessment of the relative motivational priority or urgency of the meanings or purposes of the configuration currently under study (Stolorow & Atwood, 1979). Such assessments typically change over the course of treatment and even within a single session as the functional significance of psychological configurations changes with the regressive and progressive shifts in the organization of the patient's experience, especially within the transference. In any event, the analyst should always try to interpret those meanings or purposes that are motivationally most salient and compelling at any particular juncture in the analysis. His ability to understand correctly the meanings of his patient's experiences will depend on his technical skill and knowledge, but also on the interplay between his and his patient's subjective worlds, the subject to which we now turn our attention.

TRANSFERENCE AND COUNTERTRANSFERENCE

The intersubjectivity concept developed in this chapter is a direct outgrowth of the psychoanalytic understanding of transference and countertransference. The concept of transference may be understood to refer to all the ways in which the patient's experience of the analytic relationship becomes organized according to the configurations of self and object that unconsciously structure his subjective universe. The transference is actually a microcosm of the patient's total psychological life, and the analysis of the transference provides a focal point around which the patterns dominating the patient's existence as a whole can be clarified, understood, and changed. Countertransference, in turn, refers to how the structures of the analyst's subjectivity shape his experience of the analytic relationship and, in particular, of the patient's transference.

From the continual interplay between transference and countertransference two basic situations repeatedly arise: *intersubjective conjunction* and *intersubjective disjunction*. The first of these is illustrated by instances in which the configurations of self and object structuring the patient's experiences give rise to expressions that are assimilated into closely similar central configurations in the psychological life of the analyst. Disjunction, by contrast, occurs when the analyst assimilates the material expressed by the patient into configurations that significantly alter its actual subjective meaning for the patient. Repetitive occurrences of intersubjective conjunction and disjunction are inevitable accompaniments of the analytic process and reflect the interaction of differently organized subjective worlds.

Whether or not these intersubjective situations facilitate or obstruct the progress of analysis depends in large part on the extent of the analyst's reflective self-awareness and capacity to decenter (Piaget, 1970a) from the organizing principles of his own subjective world and thereby to grasp empathically the actual meaning of the patient's experiences. When such reflective self-awareness on the part of the analyst is reliably present, then the correspondence or disparity between the subjective worlds of patient and therapist can be used to promote empathic understanding and analytic insight. In the case of an intersubjective conjunction that has been recognized, for example, the analyst may become able to find analogues in his own life of the experiences presented to him, his self-knowledge thus serving as an invaluable adjunct source of information regarding the probable background meanings of the patient's expressions. Disjunctions, once they have become conscious from a decentered perspective, may also assist the analyst's ongoing efforts to understand the patient, for then his own emotional reactions can serve as potential intersubjective indices of the configurations actually structuring the patient's experiences.

In the absence of decentered self-awareness on the part of the analyst, such conjunctions and disjunctions can seriously impede the progress of analysis. This can be seen clearly in those cases of intersubjective conjunction in which the therapist is lacking in self-awareness and becomes unconsciously so identified with his patient that he suggests or tries to impose a set of defensive solutions equivalent to those he has arrived at for himself. Depending upon their psychological compatibility, such suggestions may be embraced as fresh additions to the patient's defensive system, perhaps temporarily alleviating his suffering, but in the long run precluding the success of the analysis.

A good illustration of this situation is provided by an incident that occurred in the treatment of Fritz Perls by Wilhelm Reich (described in Perls, 1969). One of the critical factors in Perls' childhood development concerned a deeply troubled relationship with his father, who was experienced as emotionally withholding and relentlessly critical and judgmental. It appears that many of the dominating issues around which Perls' subjective life was organized concerned his need to separate himself from the powerful negative influence of his father, with whom he also became closely identified. In his autobiography Perls describes his relationship with Reich in predominantly positive terms and reports one incident that captured his imagination. This was Reich's conclusion that the man who had raised Perls was not his actual biological father, but rather that Perls was the product of relations between his mother and an uncle who was the pride of the family. Although Perls never became firmly convinced that Reich's idea was sound, he remained intrigued and confused about the possibility for the rest of his life. In view of the intense struggle to become liberated from the influence of and identification with the father, it can be easily understood why this suggestion would have struck a responsive chord, notwithstanding the fact that there was no actual evidence to support the proposition. Indeed, Perls states that he never had any idea how Reich had arrived at this conclusion.

The offering of the reconstruction becomes intelligible once we consider the historical circumstances under which the structure of *Reich's* subjective world crystallized. Reich's life was also dominated by a need to dissociate himself from the influence of his father, whose authoritarian and sexually repressive values had played a central role in provoking his beloved mother to kill herself (see Stolorow & Atwood, 1979). It was Reich's allegiance to his father and identification with his values that led him at the age of 14 to betray his mother's sexual infidelity. The father's discovery of her adultery precipitated her suicide. Reich's drastic regret and guilt over this betrayal and its tragic consequences gave rise to his lifelong struggle to overthrow authoritarianism and affirm the value of sexual freedom and spontaneity. This situation was also the source of Reich's need to deny the significance of his father in his own life, a need that culminated in his conviction that he could not possibly be his father's son. He once even went so far as to suggest that he was the offspring of his mother and a man from outer space. Such fantasies underline the degree to which he wished to dissociate himself from everything his father represented and express a defensive configuration closely resembling (though with a different origin from) the òne with which a central portion of Perls' subjective life was concerned.

A similar but less dramatic way in which intersubjective conjunction may interfere with the course of treatment is illustrated by situations in which the patient's experiences so closely correspond to those of the analyst that they are not recognized as containing psychologically significant material to be analyzed and understood. Descriptions of the patient's life that are in agreement with the analyst's personal vision of the world will accordingly tend to be regarded as reflections of objective reality rather than as manifestations of the patient's personality. Commonly, the specific region of intersubjective correspondence that escapes analytic inquiry reflects a defensive solution shared by both patient and analyst. The conjunction results in a mutual strengthening of resistance and counter-resistance and, hence, in a prolongation of the analysis.

One patient, for example, repeatedly bemoaned the mechanization and depersonalization of modern society and expressed longings for a Utopian community within which his life could have significance and meaning. His therapist, who shared this negative image of society, never responded analytically to these expressions, for they seemed to him nothing more than indicants of good reality-testing regarding the human condition. Both of them were prone to projecting the source of the difficulties in their relationships onto impersonal forces and institutions, and moreover to wishing for a world modeled on the idealized images of vanished past eras in their respective lives. The preoccupations with these images also functioned to avert a painful confrontation with certain conflictual issues concerning intimacy and dependency. The conjunction between patient and therapist here extended not only to the content of the expressed imagery, but also to aspects of its defensive purpose. The opportunity to illuminate the meanings and sources of the material, which also contained implications for the transference, was thus replaced by an unwitting, silent collusion to limit the patient's (and therapist's) attainment of self-knowledge.

Let us now consider some of the consequences that may follow from intersubjective disjunction. One immediate consequence is that the therapeutic interventions will be directed toward a subjective situation that in fact does not exist, and will tend to produce effects and reactions that from the analyst's vantage point seem incomprehensible.

A temporary intersubjective misunderstanding that developed in the treatment of another patient illustrates this dilemma. One of the origins of this patient's difficulties centered around a profound ambivalence conflict in close relationships, and more particularly around her deep conviction that her hostile feelings constituted a deadly threat to those she loved. This was vividly symbolized in the first dream she presented in treatment, in which she saw a terrifying, monstrous gorilla standing in front of a house made of delicate crystal. She experienced the people on whom she relied for support and security as fragile and vulnerable (like the crystal house), while her aggression seemed savagely destructive (like the gorilla). For her, the emergence of aggressive feelings and urges signified the danger of the *destruction and loss of objects.*

The therapist, too, had experienced difficulties with the expression of anger during her developmental years and had acquired a conviction that if she became hostile toward those she loved they would reject and hate her. In her subjective world, the emergence of aggressive feelings was associated with the danger of *loss of love.* As the patient began to structure the transference in accord with the organizing principles described earlier and began to experience anxiety over her emerging negative feelings and attitudes, the therapist assured her that the expression of anger was permissible and even desirable in the analytic relationship. Unconsciously assimilating the patient's concerns into the emotionally colored configurations of her own subjective life, she sought to give reassurance that her availability and positive interest (love) would not be withdrawn if hateful and angry feelings began to surface in the treatment. The patient rejected these reassurances and her anxiety intensified, for she was experiencing this encouragement as an invitation to disaster. The treatment foundered in this misunderstanding for several tense sessions, but began to progress again when the therapist was able to decenter from the configuration into which she had been assimilating her patient's anxiety. It then became possible to shift the focus of the interventions to a clarification of the actual meanings underlying the patient's expressions, which concerned the attribution of fragility and vulnerability to her therapist and omnipotent destructiveness to herself.

Especially damaging are the interferences with treatment that arise in consequence of protracted, unrecognized intersubjective disjunctions. In such instances, the disparity between patient and analyst can contribute to the formation of vicious countertherapeutic spirals that produce for each an ever more dramatic confrontation with dreaded scenes having salience in their respective subjective lives. Such persistent disjunctions, whereby empathy is chronically replaced by misunderstanding, invariably intensify and exacerbate the patient's suffering and manifest psychopathology. It is here that we find the source of what analysts have euphemistically termed "negative therapeutic reactions."

NEGATIVE THERAPEUTIC REACTIONS

The concept of a "negative therapeutic reaction" was created by analysts to explain those disquieting situations in which interpretations that were presumed to be correct actually made patients worse rather than better. Typically, such untoward reactions to the analyst's well-intended interpretive efforts were attributed exclusively to intrapsychic mechanisms located entirely within the mental apparatus of the patient, such as an unconscious sense of guilt, a need for punishment, and primal masochism (Freud, 1923, 1937), narcissistic character resistances (Abraham, 1919), a need to ward off the depressive position through omnipotent control (Riviere, 1936), or unconscious envy and a resulting compulsion to spoil the analytic work (Kernberg, 1975; Klein, 1957). We are contending, by contrast, that such therapeutic impasses and disasters cannot be understood apart from the intersubjective context in which they arise. They are most often the product of prolonged, unrecognized transference-countertransference disjunctions and the chronic misunderstandings that result (Brandchaft, 1983; Stolorow, Atwood & Lachmann, 1981; Stolorow & Lachmann, 1980).

Our understanding of human intersubjectivity, of the psychoanalytic situation, and of so-called negative therapeutic reactions has been deepened significantly by Kohut's (1971, 1977) concepts of selfobject and selfobject transference. In the selfobject transferences, the patient revives with the analyst the early idealizing and mirroring ties that had been traumatically and phase-inappropriately ruptured during the formative years, and upon which he now comes to rely for the restoration and maintenance of a sense of self and for the resumption and completion of arrested psychological growth. In our experience, exacerbations and entrenchments of patients' psychopathology severe enough to be termed "negative therapeutic reactions" are most often produced by prolonged unrecognized intersubjective disjunctions wherein the patient's selfobject transference needs are consistently misunderstood and thereby relentlessly rejected by the analyst. Such misunderstandings typically take the form of erroneously interpreting the revival of an arrested selfobject tie or need as an expression of malignant, pathological resistance. When the patient revives an arrested selfobject tie or need within the analytic relationship, and the analyst repeatedly interprets this developmental necessity as if it were merely a pathological resistance, the patient will experience such misinterpretations as gross failures of empathy. Consequently, traumatic psychological injuries are repeatedly inflicted, with impact similar to the pathogenic events of the patient's early life.

An example of such an unfortunate turn of events was provided by the treatment of a woman whose problems traced back to her early family's consistent failure to provide the confirming and validating responses necessary for the formation of a stable and coherent sense of self. The only exception to this pattern of relentless unresponsiveness that she could recall was her father's sexual interest in her which, according to her memories, began when she was nine years old. This had led to the cultivation of a seductive and coquettish style and ultimately to a pattern of compulsive promiscuity with father-surrogates, in a desperate effort to be recognized and counteract terrible feelings of self-depletion and self-loss.

Her therapist began her treatment in accord with his understanding of the precepts of classical psychoanalysis, which included an overly literal interpretation of the rule of abstinence. This meant that he responded to her urgent requests for affirming, mirroring responses with silence or at most a brief interpretation. She began to experience his seeming aloofness and "neutrality" as a repetition of the traumatically depriving circumstances of her childhood, and alternated in treatment beween sexualization of the transference and attempted seductions on the one hand, and expressions of deep rage on the other.

A central configuration in the therapist's subjective world concerned issues of power and control. The salience of these issues had largely arisen from a problematic childhood relationship with his mother, in which he had violently resisted submitting to what he felt was her tyrannizing and oppressive will. The dilemma around which major aspects of his subjective life were organized was the danger of relinquishing control and autonomy, which seemed to him equivalent to becoming the slave-like extension of objects. The patient's desperate demands for mirroring responsiveness were unconsciously assimilated into his emotionally charged themes of power and control, evoking a reaction of stubborn resistance and entrenching his already withholding and unresponsive style. Unaware of the countertransference reaction that had been precipitated, he envisioned his patient's intensifying demands as expressive of a malignant need for dominance. A vicious spiral was thereby set up, in which the disjunct perceptions, needs, and reactions of patient and therapist strengthened one another in a reciprocally destructive manner. The treatment continued in this situation for 18 months until it was finally terminated when the patient attemped to kill herself.

A second example of negative therapeutic reaction rooted in intersubjective disjunction occurred in the analysis of a young man who was subject to recurrent, acute states of merciless self-hatred and self-attack. His mother had clung to him parasitically as a source of emotional sustenance and had reacted to his strivings for greater separation by making him feel as if these were deliberately cruel and destructive attempts to injure her. The resulting severe impairment of his self-esteem was reflected in his lifelong search for union with an idealized maternal figure whose perfection would redeem his sense of self by transforming him from an evil being into a good one. This quest inevitably began to shape his perception of his analyst.

In the analyst's subjective world, conflicts over self-assertion and the expression of anger were prominent. Amalgamating the patient's need for an idealized selfobject to these conflictual issues of her own, the therapist consistently misinterpreted both the patient's self-attacks and idealizing attitudes as if they were expressions of a defensive splitting process that repeated early attempts to protect his mother from his own rage and aggression. The patient, in turn, experienced these interpretations as revivals of his mother's portrayals of him as inherently cruel and destructive to her, and he became increasingly immersed in hopelessness and suicidal despair. This vicious spiral was finally stemmed when supervisory interventions clarified the transference-countertransference disjunction. The supervisor demonstrated to the therapist that the motivationally most salient theme structuring the patient's subjective life at this juncture of the analysis was not a need to ward off aggression toward others, but rather a search for an archaic tie to an idealized selfobject in order to redeem his sense of self and restore self-esteem.

In examples such as these we see that chronic, unrecognized disjunctions, wherein vital developmental requirements revived in relation to the analyst meet with consistently unempathic responses, constitute the intersubjective context in which negative—often dramatically negative—"therapeutic" reactions are produced. This finding, we have come to believe, holds the broadest implications for the psychoanalytic understanding of psychopathology in general.

PSYCHOPATHOLOGY

We contend that from a psychoanalytic perspective—a perspective, that is, that derives from empathic-introspective observations from within the psychoanalytic situation—psychological disturbances can no longer be viewed as resulting solely from pathological mechanisms located within the patient. Like "negative therapeutic reactions," psychopathology in general cannot be considered apart from the intersubjective context in which it arises.

In an earlier work (Brandchaft & Stolorow, 1984), this thesis was exemplified with respect to so-called borderline psychopathology. A critique was offered of the view that the term "borderline" refers to a discrete, stable, pathological character structure rooted in pathognomonic instinctual conflicts and primitive defenses. Clinical evidence that has been cited for the centrality of such conflicts and defenses was shown actually to be evidence of needs for specific modes of relatedness to archaic selfobjects, and of the empathic failures of such selfobjects. It was proposed that the psychological essence of what is called "borderline" is not that it is a pathological condition located solely in the patient. Rather, it refers to phenomena arising in an intersubjective field—a field consisting of a precarious, vulnerable self and a failing, archaic selfobject.

When the archaic states and needs of patients who have been called borderline are correctly understood and accepted, it was claimed, they can be helped to form more or less stable selfobject transference relationships and, when this is achieved, their so-called borderline features recede and even disappear. So long as the selfobject tie to the therapist remains intact, their treatment will bear a close similarity to descriptions of analyses of narcissistic personality disorders (Kohut, 1971). When the selfobject tie to the therapist becomes significantly disrupted by empathic failures, by contrast, the patient may once again appear to be borderline. It was stressed that whether or not a stable selfobject bond can develop and be maintained, which in turn shapes both the apparent diagnostic picture and the assessment of analyzability, will not only depend on the extent of impairment and vulnerability of the patient's nuclear self. It will be codetermined as well by the extent of the therapist's ability to decenter from the structures of his own subjectivity and to comprehend empathically the nature of the patient's archaic subjective universe as it begins to structure the microcosm of the transference.

We have become convinced that through further psychoanalytic research the conception of borderline as phenomena arising and receding within an intersubjective field will be found to apply to all forms of manifest psychopathology, ranging from the psychoneurotic to the overtly psychotic. However, the intersubjective context of psychopathology is most readily demonstrated in the treatment of patients who need to rely on very archaic selfobject ties to maintain the basic structural integrity and stability of their sense of self and to prevent its structural dissolution. We now illustrate this with a case of transference psychosis.

When the patient entered treatment at the age of 25, his florid manifest psychopathology included many features that typically are termed borderline. He suffered from severe, agitated, lonely depressions and felt a desperate, devouring hunger for closeness and physical contact with women whom he experienced as awesome in their idealized qualities. At the same time, his relations with others, especially women, were extremely chaotic and sadomasochistic in nature, marked by violent rage, envy, and destructiveness directed against both objects and himself. He frequently engaged in bizarre, ritualized enactments of a sadomasochistic and sexually perverse nature.

After several months of treatment the analyst began to focus his interventions on what seemed to be an unmistakable pattern of phobic avoidance of intimate contact with women. This was understood and consistently interpreted to the patient as reflecting his intense fear of women, based on his images of them, including the maternal prototype, as terribly powerful, sadistic, and dangerously destructive. All of this was well documented in the analytic material. Indeed, the patient had disclosed that he consciously pictured the sexual act as a situation of mutual destruction and mutilation, in which his penis would inflict damage to the woman's body, and her vagina, lined with razor blades, would cut off his penis in retaliation.The patient's reaction to repeated interpretations of his phobic defense and underlying fears and fantasies was that he became intensely paranoid within the transference. He began to believe with increasing conviction that the analyst's sole motivation in making interpretations was to humiliate him, lord it over him, and ultimately destroy him. In turn, the patient became obsessed with fantasies of revenge and wishes to attack and destroy the analyst, and at times during the sessions seemed just at the brink of enacting them. Interpretations of projective mechanisms only exacerbated the patient's feelings of victimization, which eventually became entrenched in the form of full-fledged persecutory delusions.

This paranoid transference psychosis persisted for several weeks and became alleviated in large part as a consequence of two serendipitous circumstances. The first occurred when the patient inquired about a day hospital program with which he knew the analyst was familiar. The therapist responded spontaneously and nonanalytically, saying that he felt that the patient was "too together" for this particular program. The patient became utterly elated and revealed that he experienced the analyst's comment as an unexpected vote of confidence, a longed-for expression of approval. Shortly thereafter he reported a highly illuminating dream, whose symbols pointed to the emergence of archaic grandiosity and its deflation.

> I was telling people I was going to jump off of a very high altitude, a building or window sill. I wasn't going to commit suicide, I was going to jump and *live!* It would have been the first or second time in the history of the world! Then the big day came. I crawled up on the window sill and I looked down. I was scared. I couldn't jump. I saw a rope ladder and couldn't even go down that. It was incredibly humiliating. Telling people I could do something and then being too scared.

The second fortunate circumstance was that at this time the analyst was becoming acquainted with Kohut's early papers on the understanding and treatment of archaic narcissism. This new understanding was making a deep personal impact on the analyst, enabling him to expand his reflective self-awareness to include a greater knowledge of his own narcissistic vulnerabilities and needs. This expanded awareness, in turn, made it possible for him to find in his own psychological history analogues of the patient's archaic states, thereby enabling him to begin to understand the nature of the patient's selfobject transference needs and the intersubjective situation in which the transference psychosis had developed.

The patient's sense of self had been extremely vulnerable and subject to protracted fragmentations. Indeed, it was later understood, the principle purpose of his sadomasochistic, perverse enactments was to restore a tenuous sense of integrity and stability to his crumbling self-experience. What he needed, it was learned, was the opportunity to solidify a more cohesive sense of self around archaic images of perfection and omnipotence. What he most needed in the transference was to feel that the analyst appreciated and admired the grandeur of this brittle archaic self. In this specific context, the analyst's repeated interpretations of his fears of women were experienced as unendurable mortifications. The transference psychosis developed as a result of a prolonged, unrecognized intersubjective disjunction in which the therapist's interpretive approach persistently obstructed the archaic mirroring tie that the patient urgently required in order to sustain the organization of his precarious sense of self. When the disjunction was recognized, interpretively clarified, and replaced by a correct empathic comprehension of the nature of the patient's selfobject transference needs, the transference psychosis was completely dissipated, never to recur during the long course of the treatment.

THERAPEUTIC ACTION

If "negative therapeutic reactions" and psychopathology cannot be understood apart from the intersubjective contexts in which they occur, this is equally true of the therapeutic action of psychoanalysis. Freud's explanations of therapeutic action (e.g., 1914, 1937) placed the principal emphasis on intrapsychic processes, such as the patient's renunciation of infantile wishes liberated through the analysis of transference resistance. Some other analysts, however, who have attemped to account for the therapeutic action of psychoanalysis, have alluded to the importance of the intersubjective—for example, Strachey (1934) in his concept of the introjection of the analyst's benign attitudes into the patient's superego functioning, and Loewald (1960) in his stress on the patient's discovery of new modes of object relationship with the analyst.

While we would emphasize that the process of structural change always occurs in an intersubjective field, the mode of therapeutic action of this field will differ, depending on the extent to which pathological structures or remnants of insufficient structuralization predominate in the treatment at any particular juncture (see chapter 1).

When pathological structures predominate in the transference, the working-through phase and its therapeutic action can be conceptualized as a gradual process of *structural transformation:* The repeated interpretive clarification of the nature, origins, and purposes of the configurations of self and object into which the analyst is assimilated, together with the repeated juxtaposition of these patterns with experiences of the analyst as a new object to which they must accommodate, both establish reflective knowledge of how the patient's perception of the analytic relationship is being shaped by his psychological structures, and at the same time invite the synthesis of alternative modes of experiencing the self and object world. As the ossified, pathological forms that have heretofore structured the patient's experiences are progressively broken up and reorganized, a new and enriched personal reality opens up before him, made possible by the newly expanded and reflectively conscious structures of his subjective world.

Analysis thus introduces a new object into the patient's experience, an object unique in the capacity to invoke past images and yet also to demonstrate an essential difference from these early points of reference.[2] We wish to stress that the process of structural transformation does not require that the analyst play out any artificial parental or "corrective" role. The analyst's newness as an object is insured by the consistency of his observational stance—the dedication to the use of introspection and empathy to gain and provide understanding of the meaning of the patient's experiences. Every transference interpretation that successfully illuminates for the patient his unconscious past simultaneously crystallizes an illusive present—the novelty of the therapist as an understanding presence. Perceptions of self and other are perforce transformed and reshaped to allow for the new experience. Assimilation contributes the affective power inherent in the transference, while accomodation makes for change.

When remnants of faulty structuralization predominate in the transference, a different conceptualization of the working-

---

[2]Many of the ideas in this paragraph were contributed by Dr. John Munder Ross, who coauthored an earlier work on the subject of psychoanalytic treatment (Stolorow, Atwood, & Ross, 1978).

through phase and its therapeutic action is required. In such instances, the analysis aims not for the breaking up and reorganization of existing pathological structures, but rather for the growth of psychological structure that is missing or deficient as a consequence of developmental voids and interferences (Kohut, 1971, 1977; Stolorow & Lachmann, 1980). The patient is permitted to establish an archaic bond with the analyst as a selfobject and hence to revive with the analyst those early phases at which his psychological development had been arrested. When protected from traumatic disruptions, this selfobject tie serves to reinstate the developmental processes of differentiation and integration that had been aborted during the patient's formative years.

Kohut's (1971, 1977) conceptualizations of the selfobject transferences and of the central role of the analyst's empathic understanding in the establishment and working through of these transferences have brought the intersubjective context of psychoanalytic cure into particularly bold relief. He has described how the correct understanding and working through of disruptions of the selfobject bond that has been permitted to develop can result in a process of psychological structure formation. An aspect of this process that we especially wish to underscore is the patient's gradual internalization of the analyst's observational stance, whereby the quality of empathic understanding, formerly felt to be the property of the analyst as selfobject, becomes an enduring feature of the patient's own self-experience. To the therapeutic action of such transmuting internalizations we would add the mutative power of correct empathy itself. Structure-forming articulations of experience are directly promoted in the facilitating medium of the analyst's empathic communications. Thus the cumulative experience of being understood in depth leads both to the crystallization of a sense of the self that has been comprehended and to the acquisition of the capacity for empathic self-observation.

Such structuralization may be seen as proceeding through a number of steps. Repeated experiences of being understood by the analyst and the evolving perception of the analyst as a progressively more differentiated, empathically inquiring object enable the patient to form a complementary perception of himself as a person who has been and can be empathically understood. Here we see self-articulation in the medium of the analyst's understanding. Further structuralization is promoted by the repeated analysis of the patient's experiences of the absence of the analyst's empathy, which may result, for example, from misunderstandings or separations. At first the patient may fill the void by becoming able to invoke an image of the analyst's empathic responsiveness during the period of its experienced absence, thus restoring the lost feeling of being understood. During this phase, a patient undergoing a separation from the analyst may describe a feeling that the analyst is somehow "available" and "there," even though not physically present and not distinctly localized in subjective space. In such instances, the analyst crystallizes in the patient's awareness as a transitional empathic presence. Gradually, the patient comes to experience a "shift . . . from the total human context of the personality of the object to certain of its specific functions" (Kohut, 1971, p. 50). He becomes able, without needing the concrete images of the analyst, to minister the lost empathic response to himself, "not experiencing the response as from an outside source but as an integral part of the fabric of himself" (Lichtenberg, 1978). As the patient increasingly pictures himself as a person who can empathically understand himself, the internalization of the analyst's empathic qualities becomes fully integrated into the subjective self, contributing vitally to its structuralization.

It has been a conceptual error, we feel, to consider the phrase "selfobject transference" to refer to a *type* of transference characteristic of a certain type of patient. Instead, we prefer to use that phrase to refer to a *dimension* of transference—indeed, of all transference—which may fluctuate in the extent to which it occupies a position of figure or ground in the patient's experience of the analytic relationship (see Stolorow & Lachmann, 1980, ch. 9). Kohut's work has illuminated the unique therapeutic importance of understanding and working through those transference configurations in which the selfobject dimension is figure—in which, that is, the restoration or maintenance of self-experience is the paramount psychological purpose motivating the patient's specific tie to the analyst. Even when this is not the case, however, and other dimensions of experience and human motivation—such as conflicts over loving, hating, desiring, and competing—emerge as most salient in structuring the transference, the selfobject dimension is never absent. So long as it is undisturbed, preserved in the medium of the analyst's empathy, it operates silently in the background, enabling the patient to confront frightening feelings and painful dilemmas.

Consider, from this standpoint, the intersubjective situation in which a traditional resistance analysis takes place. Experienced therapists know that clarifying the nature of a patient's resistance has no discernible therapeutic result unless the analyst is also able to correctly identify the subjective danger or emotional conflict that makes the resistance a felt necessity. It is only when the analyst shows that he knows the patient's fear and anguish and thereby becomes established to some degree as a calming, containing, idealized selfobject, that the patient begins to feel safe enough to relax the resistance and allow his subjective life to emerge more freely. Every mutative therapeutic moment, even when based on interpretation of resistance and conflict, derives its therapeutic action from the intersubjective field in which it occurs.

From the standpoint of a theoretical framework that takes the structure of a person's experiencing as its central focus, the often-raised question of whether the treatment of emotional conflicts (pathological structures) and of developmental arrests (failures of structuralization) require two entirely separate psychoanalytic systems is moot. Psychoanalytic phenomenology, conceived as a depth psychology of human subjectivity, is sufficiently inclusive to encompass and guide the treatment of both emotional conflict and developmental arrest.

CONCLUSIONS

Psychoanalytic treatment may be viewed as a set of facilitating conditions that permit the structure of a patient's subjective universe to unfold maximally and find illumination in relatively pure culture in the analytic transference. From the perspective of psychoanalytic phenomenology, clinical phenomena such as transference and countertransference, negative therapeutic reactions, psychopathology in general, and the therapeutic action of psychoanalysis cannot be understood apart from the intersubjective contexts in which they take form. Patient and analyst together form an indissoluble psychological system, and it is this system that constitutes the empirical domain of psychoanalytic inquiry.

3   INTERSUBJECTIVITY: II. DEVELOPMENT AND PATHOGENESIS

(Written in Collaboration with Bernard Brandchaft)

Winnicott once remarked, "There is no such thing as an infant" (quoted in Winnicott, 1965, p. 39), meaning that infant and maternal care together form an indivisible unit. Having in the previous chapter developed a similar argument with regard to the psychoanalytic patient, we now extend our intersubjective perspective in the direction suggested by Winnicott's evocative remark. We contend that both psychological development and pathogenesis are best conceptualized in terms of the specific intersubjective contexts that shape the developmental process and that facilitate or obstruct the child's negotiation of critical developmental tasks and successful passage through developmental phases. The observational focus is the evolving psychological field constituted by the interplay between the differently organized subjectivities of child and caretakers (Loewald, 1970).

This observational stance is, in our view, a fundamental methodological requirement for investigating changes occuring within the subjective world of any party within the developmental system. We stress, as Sander (1975) also stresses in regard to his studies of infants, that this stance is different from the more traditional psychoanalytic one in that the questions asked, the route of discovery, the window into the unconscious and to ontogeny, and the understandings that become possible are all different.

An "interactionist" perspective, combining "nature" with "nurture," has long been advocated by developmental theorists. Erikson (1950), for example, in line with Hartmann's (1939) developmental concept of "fitting together," conceived of the laws of epigenesis as creating "a succession of potentialities for significant interaction" with the environment (p. 67). In a statement anticipating much current thinking in the area of infancy research, he argued that "whatever reaction patterns are given biologically and whatever schedule is predetermined developmentally must be considered to be a series of *potentialities for changing patterns of mutual regulation*" (p. 69; italics in original). In a similar vein, Waddington (1957) postulated that human personality is a

> structure that develops unceasingly along one or another of an array of possible and discrete pathways. All pathways are thought to start close together so that, at conception, an individudal has access to a large range of pathways along any one of which he might travel. The one chosen turns at each and every stage on an interaction between the organism as it has developed up to that moment and the environment in which it then finds itself (quoted in Bowlby, 1981, p. 248).

Describing the interaction between nature and nurture in the infant-mother dyad, Mahler (1968) wrote that:

> infants present a large variety of cues . . . . . In a complex manner, the mother responds selectively to only *certain* of these cues. The infant gradually alters his behavior in relation to this selective response; he does so in a characteristic way—the resultant of his own innate endowment and the mother-child relationship. From this circular interaction emerge patterns of behavior that already show certain overall qualities of the child's personality . . . . It is the specific unconscious need of the mother that activates, out of the infant's infinite potentialities, those in particular that create for each mother "the child" who reflects her own *unique* and individual needs (pp. 18–19; see also Lichtenstein, 1961).

While an interactionist perspective is not new to developmental theory, the concept of intersubjectivity brings into sharpened focus the particular domain of interaction between child and environment that is most important for psychoanalysis—the unique interplay between the vulnerable, evolving subjectivity of the child and the more complexly organized and firmly consolidated subjectivities of caretakers (Loewald,1978). Thus the intersubjective perspective closes the gap between those (e.g., Sullivan, 1953) who stress the social determinants of personality development and those who emphasize the private world of impulse, fantasy, feeling, and thought.

Findings from a number of highly sophisticated research studies of the micro-interactions between the infant and its caretakers (reviewed in Beebe, in press, and Lichtenberg, 1981) are lending strong support to the claim that the organization of behavior must be viewed as "the property of the infant-environment system" of mutual regulation (Sander, 1976). These studies are beginning to spell out in detail the precise nature of the sensorimotor "dialogue" (Spitz, 1964) that results from the interplay between the psychological structures of infant and caretaker. Microkinesic movie analyses, for example, reveal that "the choreography of the behavioral 'dance' between mother and infant" consists of "split-second reciprocal adjustments of behavior completed within seconds or fractions of seconds, with a discernible structure or 'rules' of mutual regulation" (Beebe, in press). The exquisite synchronization and "enduringly harmonious coordination" (Sander, 1977, p. 136) of these split-second mutual adjustments (Stern, 1971) lead some researchers to conclude that the bond between mother and infant should be viewed as a system of joint participation in shared organizational forms (Condon & Sander, 1974). Beebe (in press) suggests that the temporal patterning of this "interlocking responsivity" and "fine-grained attunement" provides the context in which psychic structuralization takes place (see also Stern, 1983). Like Spitz (1964), she finds that "proto-defensive activity" (e.g., withdrawal) occurs when disturbances in this finely tuned reciprocal regulation result in derailments of the sensorimotor dialogue between infant and caretaker.

As we stated in the previous chapter, our understanding of the intersubjective nature of the psychoanalytic situation has been deepened significantly by Kohut's (1971, 1977) conceptualization of the selfobject tranferences, wherein the patient comes to require the analyst's understanding and empathic responsiveness for the restoration and maintenance of a sense of self and for the resumption of arrested psychological growth. We agree with Schwaber's (1979) suggestion that the selfobject concept offers a unique bridge between the fields of psychoanalytic and infant observation (see also Basch, in press). The selfobject concept provides a depth-psychological framework for understanding the developmental significance—e.g., for the epigenesis and structuralization of self-experience—of the exquisitely coordinated reciprocal regulatory patterns disclosed by infancy researchers. More generally, it brings into bold relief the profoundly intersubjective nature of human development in every phase of the life cycle.

Wolf (1980) alludes to this point in his outline of the early stages of the "developmental line of selfobject relations," wherein "the infant experiences the parent and the parent experiences the infant as an essential aspect of the well-being of the self—as selfobject" (p. 122). The cumulative effect of "a history of finely attuned reciprocal responses . . . gradually [transforms] baby and mother into custom-fitted parts of a unique mother-child unit. Both experience themselves as part of this unit that imparts strength to their individual selves through a kind of merger" (p. 124).

The conceptualization of an intersubjective field is, in part, an attempt to lift the selfobject concept to a higher, more inclusive level of generality. It is our view that the selfobject concept needs to be significantly broadened in order to describe adequately the specific unfolding developmental needs of a particular child and how these are assimilated by the psychological world of each caretaker. Kohut (1983) seemed to suggest something similar when he remarked,

> We also realize what an enormous field for further research has opened up before us, challenging us to bring further order into not a small group of monotonously similar phenomena and explanations but, on the contrary, an almost overwhelming multiplicity of possibilities . . . . [It is our task] to formulate an optimum number of explanatory clusters of specific selfobject failures and of their specific results (pp. 401–402).

We are contending that *every* phase in a child's development is best conceptualized in terms of the unique, continuously changing psychological field constituted by the intersection of the child's evolving subjective universe with those of caretakers. With the aid of a broadened selfobject concept, we can begin to formulate in detail the specific intersubjective contexts in which this progression occurs, and in which particular developmental steps are taken and developmental phases traversed. Pathogenesis, from this intersubjective perspective, is understood in terms of severe disjunctions or asynchronies that occur between the structures of subjectivity of parents and child, whereby the child's primary developmental needs do not meet with the requisite responsiveness from selfobjects. When the psychological organization of the parent cannot sufficiently accomodate to the changing, phase-specific needs of the developing child, then the more malleable and vulnerable psychological structure of the child will accomodate to what is available. A number of pathological outcomes are possible. The child may develop a defensive "false self" (Winnicott, 1960), an "identity theme" (Lichtenstein, 1961) that serves the archaic selfobject needs of the parent, in order to maintain the needed tie at whatever cost to authentic self-experience (Miller, 1979). Or the child may employ distancing as a permanent protective shield, or develop symptoms in which sequestered nuclei of an archaic self are preserved in conflict with, or in isolation from, the unresponsive selfobjects.

We wish to stress that from the beginning each developmental phase prepares each party for the new and more complex succeeding phase, for the emergence of a new intersubjective field, determining for the child which pathways lie open and which have been foreclosed. This is seen particularly clearly in the prenatal stage, but it is equally true for each succeeding phase. The preparation for the embryo to emerge as neonate depends in large part upon the interplay between its biological system and innate developmental patterning and that of the mother. The mother's preparation is also profoundly influenced by the specific psychological *meanings* the newcomer has for her as her experience of the pregnancy is assimilated into the already existing structure of her sense of self, including especially, her body-self. To harbor within her body a new living and parasitic entity with its absolute dependence, to have her body change radically in ways that cannot be controlled, to realize that her life will never again be the same and now contains a new and central uncertainty—all of these changes require significant reorganization of her subjective world. The most glaring instances of failure in this task of restructuring are seen in the syndrome of post-partum depression.

What is evident in this initial phase applies to every succeeding one as well. Ordinarily the intersubjective field within which the developmental process unfolds is a tripartite one from the beginning, with the father and his reactions having a profound impact on the mother's experience of herself and her baby. In cases of severe post-partum depression, for example, an important contributing factor can be the mother's fear that she and the child will be disappointments to the father. The factors that determine the outcome of the crucial prenatal and postnatal reorganizations are prototypes that herald later events. The mother may react to the birth of her child as a loss of a significant part of herself, or to the infant's needs as threats to her own insufficiently established self-boundaries. She may react to the birth as a loss of her own central position with her husband, or she may react to her husband's loss of *her* as a primary selfobject. Any and all such factors may result in a weakened and unsupported sense of self in the mother, leading to rigidity, distancing, and other interferences in her function, and contributing from the beginning to a constricted field in which initial psychological patternings are thrown out of kilter and the child's development impeded. A mother with a precarious sense of self may later come to rely on the child to serve her own unfulfilled archaic selfobject needs. Thereupon she will experience the child's inevitable shortcomings as indicators of fatal flaws in her own self and his strivings for greater autonomy as threats to the vitally needed tie.

The remainder of this chapter is devoted to three developmental tasks or crises that have received considerable attention in the clinical psychoanalytic literature and that frequently appear in genetic reconstructions derived from psychoanalytic treatment of adults—the subjective differentiation of self from primary object, the integration of affectively discrepant experiences of self and others, and the passing of the oedipal period. In discussions of these milestones offered by those who consider them to be central in personality development—e.g., Mahler et al. (1975), Kernberg (1976), and Freud (1924), respectively—the principal emphasis has been on the vicissitudes of drive and defense and other intrapsychic mechanisms presumed to be involved. Our efforts, in contrast, focus on the specific intersubjective contexts that facilitate or obstruct the child's negotiation of these developmental tasks. For each, we provide a clinical illustration of developmental failure, as reconstructed from an intersubjective viewpoint.

SELF-OBJECT DIFFERENTIATION

A requirement for the child's achievement and consolidation of self-object differentiation and of stable self-boundaries is the presence of a mirroring selfobject who, by virtue of a demarcated and firmly structured sense of self and others, is able reliably to recognize, affirm, appreciate, and pridefully enjoy the unique qualities and independent strivings of the child. When a parent cannot recognize and affirm central qualities and strivings of the child, because they conflict with a need for that child to serve the parent's own archaic selfobject needs, then the child will experience disturbances of self in the area of unmirrored grandiosity, as Kohut (1971, 1977) has shown. We wish to stress that such pathogenic intersubjective situations in addition will seriously obstruct the process of self-object differentiation and self-boundary formation, as the child feels compelled to "become" the selfobject that the parent requires and thus to subjugate any striving to develop according to his own separate design.

Clinical Illustration

When first seen in analysis, Amy was a 33-year-old professional woman. She was attractive, with chestnut hair and a graceful walk, which contributed to an ethereal air about her, as if she never quite touched the ground. She was the mother of three children and the wife of a prominent man active in politics and corporate business. As a professional, mother, and wife, she performed all her duties in exemplary manner, with characteristic modesty and almost without complaint. She had so arranged her schedule that her professional activities rarely interfered with her domestic interests and duties. She did not know exactly why she had entered analysis, as all the things she had hoped for when she was growing up had in fact come to pass. Nor could any of her friends believe she needed analysis, since they regarded her as the most normal person they knew and her family as the very paradigm of what a family should be. From the very first session she expressed the feeling that there was something "not quite right" about her, but even when encouraged she could not articulate exactly what it was or why she felt that way. Later she was able to articulate a sense of being perpetually child-like and unformed, together with a painful feeling of not really existing. Her childhood memories seemed like isolated episodes or pieces surrounded by "blanks," with no sense of continuity of being. She frequently asserted that the analyst would have to tell her when she had completed the analysis, because otherwise she would have no way of knowing.

As the analysis progressed, her ethereal air and quality of vagueness, especially in relation to any transference feelings, became more marked. For many years she made no direct, emotionally significant reference to the existence of the analyst. There were no direct indications of any alteration of her mood when anticipating separations from him, except for what appeared to be slightly compulsive and excited efforts to schedule additional time with her family. Over long periods she spoke unceasingly of her daily activities, especially of her interactions with her children, in whose moods and pursuits she seemed completely immersed. Only gradually did it become apparent that in this mode of being with the analyst she protected herself against a diffuse vulnerability in ways that had become unquestioned aspects of her character.

Her relationships were marked by a pervasive characteristic—to be pleasing, to do what was expected and like it, and above all, not to offend. It was a matter of pride to her that she was able to get anyone she chose to like her, and of equal importance that she be able to "understand" how she was at fault if someone she cared about were displeased with her. She explained that she could not do anything about another's reaction, but she could always improve her own behavior. It became clear that she so much centered herself around the goals, needs, and wishes of her husband, children,and friends—around what she "should" do, say, think, and feel—that she often could not discern what she actually felt or what her own inclination might be. Her distancing from the analyst was therefore the only way she felt she could preserve any sense of self of her own.

With her children she knew only too well what perfect mothering should be. However, so indistinct were her boundaries from theirs, that she experienced their every setback, every hurt, every disappointment as if it were her own, and organized its meaning for them exactly as it would be for her.

A distinct pattern eventually emerged in the transference. So long as the analyst contented himself with acknowledgments and summaries of what she had said, the relationship seemed smooth, conjunctive, and harmonious. However, the slightest shift in emphasis or expansion beyond the specific points of her communication produced a disturbance in cadence, a temporary dysrythmia that she needed to set right. She was at first unaware of the "out-of-kilter" alteration that had preceded her attempts to restore harmony. Gradually, it became clear that the patient was attempting to use the analytic situation to begin a process of differentiation and demarcation of her self-boundaries by focusing on her own perceptions and subjective experiences and articulating them. The analyst's only role was to provide the facilitating medium in which this could occur. For many years any attempt to go beyond these limits was felt as intrusive upon her self-experience, the reality and solidity of which she needed desperately to have strengthened. Such intrusions raised the threat of dissolution of her emerging self-boundaries and the fear of the analyst's perceptions and organizing principles usurping her own.

Gradually the patient came to understand the origins of the weakness in her self-boundaries. Initially she had described her relationship with her mother in ideal terms. No child had ever

had a more understanding and loving mother than she. Their relationship was the envy of her friends, as her mother prided herself in her ability to be accepted, not as a parent, but as "one of
the girls." Her father was hard-working and, although there was
no question of his love for her, he left the matter of her care entirely in the hands of his wife. The influence of her mother was, in
crucial areas, extremely subtle and therefore very difficult to sort
out. One characteristic that appeared repeatedly in the analytic
material was her mother's extreme vulnerability to hurt if Amy
disobeyed or disappointed her. But her mother would steadfastly
disclaim these reactions, thereby depriving Amy of needed support for the development of confidence in her autonomous perceptions and judgments. Additionally, her mother would frequently
explain Amy's perceptions as if they were part of the "normal"
difficulty that mothers have to go through at various times in the
development of their daughters; i.e., as if this essential building
block of self-differentiation were a transient aberration, a "stage"
to be outgrown.

The mother could not understand, for example, why Amy when
in her teens would fail to appreciate her buying dresses for her.
The dresses were exactly what the mother would have chosen for
herself, or would have wished her own mother to have chosen for
her. In this, the mother demonstrated her inability to recognize,
affirm, and validate her daughter's own developing tastes, separate and distinct from those of the mother herself. Her mother
also suffered a thousand deaths whenever the patient was upset
or acutely unhappy. Just as she could not allow her daughter to
have perceptions or tastes of her own, so she could not permit her
to have moods of her own. She would react to the patient's unhappiness as if it were her own total failure. If her daughter disliked
herself, the mother would leave no stone unturned to try to fix it.
The patient recalled that her mother's reactions to her dysphoric
moods were much more oppressive than her own unhappy feelings. It gradually became clear to Amy that her mother desperately needed her to be an ideal child in order to maintain her own
tenuous self-esteem. Any imperfection in Amy's state of mind or
performance her mother experienced as an exposure of her own
flawed self.

The obstruction of self-boundary development occurred subtly, but was relentless in its effect. "Don't you hate people who have to wear designer's medals on the backs of their jeans just because everyone else is wearing them?" her mother would ask, and Amy would immediately feel that she would never want to be such a person. At age 11, the patient already knew what kind of wedding she was going to have. "A wedding," her mother told her, "is supposed to be a private celebration of two people and a few close friends and family, not a circus held to show how many people you know," and Amy's turned out to be exactly so. It was no accident that she had the same number of children as her mother. One of Amy's differentiated, authentic yearnings was her persistent wish for just one more child.

In summary, this patient's psychopathology can be seen as stemming from an arrest in the development of self-object differentiation and self-boundaries. This deficit was manifest most noticably in her difficulty with the perception and articulation of her own subjective experience, and her inability to center herself around that experience and hence to initiate action according to some design of her own. This difficulty was found to be the consequence of her mother's need for Amy to serve as an idealized reflection of her own self and her resulting inability to recognize, affirm, and validate the patient's emergent sense of being a distinct and demarcated person, and of her father's unavailability as a selfobject with whom this developmental thrust might have been engaged collaterally. Amy adapted by attempting to become the idealized selfobject that her mother required, sacrificing those elements of the self-differentiating process that posed a threat to this archaic tie. Thus the arrested self-object differentiation seemed not to be the product of a "symbiotic fixation," of conflicts over the aggression inherent in separating (though such conflicts were not absent), or of any other such intrapsychic mechanism. It resulted instead from the absence, during critical developmental phases, of an intersubjective context in which a differentiated self-definition could be crystallized and consolidated. It was just such a facilitating context that the patient sought in the analytic transference.

INTEGRATION OF AFFECTIVELY DISCREPANT EXPERIENCES

A requirement for the child's attainment of the capacity to synthesize affectively contrasting experiences of self and others is the presence of a holding, containing selfobject who, by virtue of firmly integrated perceptions, is able reliably to accept, tolerate, comprehend, and eventually render intelligible the child's intense, contradictory affective states as issuing from a unitary, continuous self. When a parent, in contrast, must perceive the child as "split"—e.g., into one being whose "good" affects meet the selfobject needs of the parent and a second, alien being whose "bad" affects frustrate those needs—then the development of the child's integrative capacity will be severely impeded as affectively discrepant experiences of self and others become enduringly sequestered from one another in conformity with the parent's fragmentary perceptions.

Clinical Illustration[1]

Linda, an attractive, stylish 25-year-old woman who worked as an office manager, entered treatment with a variety of psychosomatic and psychological problems, including ulcers, chronic neck and back pain, migraine headaches, tightness of the jaw, feelings of extreme self-consciousness and depersonalization, and states of severe, empty depression accompanied by suicidal fantasies. She spoke of past involvements with men that had ended disastrously for her, leaving her feeling unbearably rejected and hurt. She had tried to protect herself from this by erecting barriers against any emotional involvements, and had isolated herself from men for more than a year. Now she felt walled in, numb, and lifeless, and feared that she was losing control over her mind and body and was about to "break down from circuit overload."

From the start Linda showed great reluctance to become immersed in the analytic process. After postponing the beginning of

---

[1] We are grateful to Dr. Richard Ulman for providing us with this illustrative case material.

treatment for several weeks, she "forgot" the first session. When she finally did begin, she insisted that she could not think or talk spontaneously about herself or her problems, and that she needed suggestions from the analyst as to what topics to cover. Initially she could recall almost nothing of her childhood and adolescent years, and she would become "blocked" whenever the therapeutic dialogue seemed to be leading her toward a strong feeling. Exploration of these early resistances disclosed her need for absolute control of her emotions and her terror that any loosening of her affective life would result in her going completely berserk.

Gradually, she began to remember and reveal how miserable and unhappy she had been as a child and how sad and suicidal she had felt as an adolescent. Her mother emerged in her memories as a cold and unexpressive woman who had little time for Linda because she "had her hands full" with an alcoholic and violent husband, two disobedient older children, two toddlers, and her own assortment of physical ailments. The mother seemed always focused on the negative, constantly pointing up Linda's shortcomings. The patient recalled that she had been "scared to death" of her father, who regularly came home in a drunken stupor, terrorizing the family with explosive outbursts of temper. Having witnessed the damage that her two older siblings had sustained in trying to confront their father, Linda chose instead to keep all her feelings inside.

Two dreams illuminated aspects of the transference during this early period of treatment. In the first, Linda was talking with her roommate when suddenly a horrible, ugly, deformed old man burst through an open window and came at them in a menacing way. In the second, Linda went to her pharmacist and asked him to fill a prescription for a pain killer, but was worried that he would refuse her request. The first dream and the patient's associations revealed her fear that the analyst, like her father, would destructively break into her subjective world and wreak havoc therein. The second indicated her need for accepting, calming, soothing responses from the analyst, as well as her fear that he would reject this need as her mother had.

Something new began to emerge in the transference. Typically she would describe some emotionally charged experience in her current life, and then turn to the analyst and ask, "What do *you* think?" On one such occasion she said that she could see nothing about herself with her own mind's eye, whereas the analyst, she imagined, knew everything that was going on inside her. Initially the analyst misunderstood the meaning of her questions, believing them to be an expression of an idealizing transference. Later he and the patient came to understand that the questions served a defensive purpose, reflecting Linda's profound distrust of her own perceptions and feelings and her deep fear that these would not be tolerated by the analyst.

The patient began to remember and reconstruct a recurrent trauma that she experienced in her relationship with her mother beginning at age four and continuing until she was eight. Whenever Linda showed any intense feelings—particularly dysphoric, critical, angry, or defiant feelings—her mother would not only scold and punish her; she would act as if her daughter had literally metamorphosed into an entirely different person, an alien and evil intruder, and would even refer to her repeatedly by a fictitious name, "Joanne." In consequence of this cumulative trauma, a deep division was perpetuated in Linda's self-experience. On the one hand she was the emotionally inhibited, compliant, perfectly behaved good little girl who satisfied her mother's need for an idealized self-extension. On the other hand, particularly when strong affect stirred within her, she was the sinister Joanne whom her mother could not tolerate and who, like her father, might at any moment violently and uncontrollably erupt. The consequences of this inner fragmentation were states of depersonalization and severe identity confusion, the distrust of her own perceptions and feelings and the use of regressed (psychosomatic) pathways of affect expression, a conviction that there was something terribly "wrong" and "abnormal" about her, and pervasive feelings of inherent badness, worthlessness, and self-loathing.

Linda's unintegrated self-experiences, we wish to stress, did not appear to be the product of any defensive splitting process designed to ward off ambivalence. They arose instead from her attempts to adapt to her mother's fragmentary perceptions of her and from the absence, during a critical period of her childhood, of an intersubjective context in which opposing affective states could be synthesized and come to be experienced as issuing from a unitary, continuous self. In the transference she sought this context in the form of a longed-for holding, containing selfobject who would recognize, tolerate, and affirm the subjective validity of her intense, often contradictory feelings.

THE PASSING OF THE OEDIPAL PERIOD

The intersubjective context of the child's passage through the oedipal phase has been described in some detail by Kohut (1977) in terms of two ways in which the child's oedipal self-experience may be assimilated by the structure of the parents' subjective worlds:

> The affectionate desire and the assertive-competitive rivalry of the oedipal child will be responded to by normally empathic parents in two ways. The parents will react to the sexual desires and to the competitive rivalry of the child by becoming sexually stimulated and counteraggressive, and, at the same time, they will react with joy and pride to the child's developmental achievement, to his vigor and assertiveness (p. 230).

Whether the impact of the oedipal period will be growth enchancing or pathogenic will depend on the balance that the child experiences between these two modes of parental response:

> If the little boy, for example, feels that his father looks upon him proudly as a chip off the old block and allows him to merge with him and with his adult greatness, then his oedipal phase will be a decisive step in self-consolidation and self-pattern-firming, including the laying down of one of the several variants of integrated maleness . . . . If, however, this aspect of the parental echo is absent during the oedipal phase, the child's oedipal conflicts will, even in the absence of grossly distorted parental responses to the child's libidinal and aggressive strivings, take on a malignant quality. Distorted parental responses are, moreover, also likely to occur under these circumstances. Parents who are not able to establish empathic contact with the developing self of the child will, in other words, tend to see the constituents of the child's oedipal

aspirations in isolation—they will tend to see . . . alarming sexuality and alarming hostility in the child instead of larger configurations of assertive affection and assertive competition—with the result that the child's oedipal conflicts will become intensified (pp.
234–235).

Thus, from this perspective, even the tempestuous
neurotogenic sexual and aggressive conflicts and compromises of
the oedipus complex cannot be understood apart from the
intersubjective contexts—the selfobject failures—in which they
take form.

Clinical Illustration

Jonathan, a 43-year-old real estate developer and father of two
children, sought treatment for premature ejaculation. He had experienced this problem episodically throughout his 18-year-
marriage, but it had worsened considerably in recent weeks, during a time of major successes for him in business. He indicated
that his newfound feelings of accomplishment were creating tensions in his relationships with his wife and his older brother,
making it difficult for him to continue to accept the subordinate
role that he had always assumed with them both.

Jonathan quickly immersed himself in analysis with a vigor
and enthusiasm that rarely waned throughout the course of treatment. He seemed to hang on every word from the analyst, and at
the same time became increasingly expansive in his own self-
expression. After some preliminary exploration of his feeling that
it was "obligatory" that he endlessly satisfy and please his wife,
which paralleled what he had felt with his mother, the premature
ejaculations ceased, though the problem would recur whenever
the therapeutic bond became significantly disrupted.

Further exploration of the imperative that he please his wife
disclosed Jonathan's nuclear sense of himself as castrated,
unmanly, hopelessly inadequate, and unable to compete with
other men. The genetic origins of this self-perception unfolded
over the four-year course of the analysis.

At first, the patient traced his feelings of being flawed and
unmanly to his adolescence, when he was cruelly teased and hu-

miliated by peers because his genitals were late in developing. Soon, however, his associations began to coalesce around memories of his relationship with his brother, which would dominate the treatment during the early months. The brother, four years older and highly talented in art and music, seemed always at the center of their parents' attention, with Jonathan feeling perpetually in his shadow. Since he felt that he himself lacked any talent worthy of recognition, the patient tried to win his parents' approval by helping his mother, being compliant and dependable, a "goodie-two-shoes"—the role to which his relationship with his wife later became heir. As his parents often seemed too preoccupied with their marital problems to be concerned with him, from the age of five or six he increasingly turned for guidance and direction to his brother, adulating him and believing him to be in possession of "oracular" powers. His brother was quite competitive and often bullied and humiliated him, but Jonathan could never fight back because of the enormity of his need for the tie. Only now, in the wake of the patient's own undeniable achievements, was the brother's exalted position being called into question.

Eventually it emerged that behind Jonathan's idealizing tie to his brother lay a desperate yearning for recognition from his father, a yearning that had been doomed to recurrent, traumatic disappointment. The father, a bitterly unfulfilled man himself, saw in his older son the embodiment of his own frustrated artistic aspirations, and thus seemed perpetually to shower him with attention, encouragement, and praise. In his younger boy, however, he could see only his own weaknesses and failures, his own disappointing and debased self, and thus he responded consistently to Jonathan's competitive ambitions and artistic efforts with disinterest, belittlement, and contempt. The patient recovered an early memory from the age of five or six that seemed to encapsulate the numerous, repetitive injuries that resulted from the father's inability to respond with pride and pleasure to his son's expanding oedipal-phase self. Jonathan had spent hours at an aunt's house painting a large, ambitious picture (it was only away from home and in secret that he dared to venture into his brother's artistic domain). His father walked in and asked who had done it. When the aunt replied that it was Jonathan, the father quipped, "that figures," and walked away in disgust. The patient became resigned that he could gain his father's recognition and thus acquire a modicum of self-worth and support for his masculine self only "by proxy," through feeling connected to the brother who seemed to embody all that their father admired.

Later in the analysis a still deeper injury to the patient's phallic-oedipal self was uncovered, this time in relation to his mother. Jonathan's oedipal years were clouded by nearly constant strife between his parents and recurrent scenes in which the father would angrily accuse the mother of infidelity and the mother would then dissolve in tears. When his mother cried, the patient recalled, he felt her pain within himself and became devoted to relieving her anguish. He began to remember and understand the extent to which his mother had turned to him for solace and consolation, for soothing and comforting, and how her need for him had required that an archaic sense of oneness between them be maintained, at whatever cost to his own growth into boyhood and manhood. The closest times were when he was ill and they could share their miseries together, his physical and hers emotional. The maintenance of this symbioticlike bond precluded any responsiveness on the part of the mother to the boy's developing separateness and, especially, to his phallic-oedipal self. Hence what seemed the deepest source of his self-perception as castrated and unmasculine was disclosed—the profound absence of a maternal mirror for his emerging, self-assertive, phallic-grandiose, oedipal-phase boyishness.

In summary of this clinical illustration, the intersubjective context of Jonathan's failure to successfully traverse the oedipal phase was quite complex, entailing three interrelated aspects and their corresponding aborted developmental thrusts. At the core was his mother's need for oneness with the boy as a soothing, comforting, archaic selfobject and her consequent inability to provide any mirroring responsiveness to his emerging phallic grandiosity and oedipal assertiveness. When the patient turned to his father as a compensatory oedipal selfobject, he too could not supply the requisite mirroring responsiveness, seeing the boy only as a replica of his own deficient, despised self. Jonathan's last recourse was to seek union with his older brother, whom his father admired as the possessor of idealized artistic qualities, as an indirect source of self-esteem and masculine strength. But because of the brother's competitiveness, the price of maintaining this sorely needed tie was further subjugation and constriction of the patient's own self-development.

In the analysis this three-step genetic sequence unravelled in reverse order. At first, contact with the analyst as an idealized "oracular" brother-figure was sufficient to elevate the patient's self-confidence (and remove his symptom). Next to unfold was his need for the analyst to serve as a paternal selfobject who would recognize his considerable talents and affirm his competitive ambitions and achievements. Last to emerge was his deep, arrested need (experienced primarily with his wife, but also with the analyst) for the absent maternal mirroring of his phallic grandiosity, his wish for the unconditional adoration of his strengths and masculine prowess that would make him feel that he could "move mountains" and "vanquish all rivals."

CONCLUSIONS

Every stage in a child's development is best conceptualized psychoanalytically in terms of the unique, continuously changing psychological field constituted by the intersection of the child's evolving subjective universe with those of caretakers. This observational stance brings into sharpened focus the specific intersubjective contexts that shape the developmental process and that facilitate or obstruct the child's negotiation of developmental tasks and passage through developmental phases. Three critical developmental tasks—the differentiation of self from object, the integration of affectively discrepant experiences, and the passing of the oedipal period—are examined from this intersubjective perspective, along with a clinical illustration of developmental failure in each area. In each case it was seen that the patient sought to establish in the analytic transference the requisite facilitating intersubjective context that had been absent or insufficient during the formative years and that now permitted the arrested developmental process to resume.

4   PATHWAYS OF
       CONCRETIZATION

We have proposed, as a supraordinate principle of human motivation, that the need to maintain the organization of experience is a central motive in the patterning of human action (see chapter 1). The basic psychological process that mediates this functional relationship between experience and action is *concretization*—the encapsulation of structures of experience by concrete, sensorimotor symbols. We have come to believe that the concretization of experience is a ubiquitous and fundamental process in human psychological life and that it underlies a great variety of psychological activities and products. Concretization can assume a number of forms, depending on what pathways or modes of expression it favors. For example, when motor activity predominates in the mode of concretization, then behavioral enactments are relied upon to actualize required configurations of experience. When motor activity is curtailed, as in sleep, then perceptual imagery may become the preferred pathway of concretization, as in dreams.

In this chapter we provide illustrative material that we hope will indicate the wide scope of the concretization principle and the broad range of psychological phenomena it encompasses. We begin with brief examples of neurotic symptoms, because this is

where psychoanalysis first discovered the centrality of unconscious symbolization. Next we offer an expanded formulation of
the concept of the transitional object. In the final two sections we
present more extensive discussions of enactments and dreams. In
our clinical illustrations we seek to identify the specific configurations of experience that these varied psychological phenomena
concretize and thereby to demonstrate the diversity of personal
purposes served by this ubiquitous process. Wherever possible,
we   examine   the   intersubjective   contexts   in   which   the
concretization products arise and recede.

NEUROTIC SYMPTOMS

The early psychoanalytic discovery that hysterical conversion
symptoms and other neurotic inhibitions could be resolved by unveiling their unconscious *meanings* (Breuer & Freud, 1893–1895)
was perhaps the first major demonstration of the role of
concretization in the genesis of psychopathological constellations.
However, in resorting to metapsychological notions of crypto-
physiological energy transformations to explain this phenomenon, Freud and others obscured the important finding that the
use of concrete, sensorimotor symbolism was central to the process of symptom formation. As this phenomenon is by now well
known, two brief examples will suffice.

Midway through the course of her four-year analysis, a
33-year-old woman reported a new symptom—a tightening of or
lump in her throat, with difficulty swallowing. During the session
she indicated that she had recently experienced some competitive
successes in relation to a number of other women, and that she
felt vaguely uneasy about this. Her associations around this
theme eventually led to memories of how unbearably guilty she
had felt as a child whenever she would present some personal triumph to her chronically depressed mother, who always seemed so
pathetic, so emotionally crippled, so painfully unfulfilled. "Whenever I brought home an 'A' from school," she said, "it was like
shoving my success down my mother's throat." The analyst interpreted that in the new symptom she seemed to be doing to her

own throat what she feared her successes might do to her mother's. This single interpretation of the symptom's unconscious meaning as a "symbol written in the sand of the flesh" (Lacan, 1953, p. 69) was sufficient to remove it permanently. In this case the sensorimotor symbolism of the throat encapsulated her sense of guilt over the injury her success might inflict on her mother, and the concretization served the purposes of atonement and self-punishment.

A 28-year-old man (whose treatment was briefly mentioned in Stolorow & Atwood, 1979, chapter 6) sought treatment in order to restore some emotional spontaneity to his regimented life and to correct the sexual inhibitions from which he suffered. He explained to his therapist that he believed that he possessed a limited supply of energy and bodily fluids that he had to conserve, and that he could permit himself to have sexual relations only during the weekends for fear that sexual activity on weekdays would so drain him of these substances that he would have insufficient amounts of them left over for the performance of his work. Further exploration of his fear of being drained revealed that in the sexual situation he experienced his wife, much as he had experienced his mother, as a "bottomless pit" of never-ending needs and demands that he, perforce, was required to satisfy. The imagery of dwindling energies and fluids symbolically encapsulated his dread of dissipating himself in servitude to the appetites of a mother-surrogate, and the concretization served a self-protective function in providing him with a feeling of control—he believed that he could conserve his energies and fluids and thereby protect against loss of self by constricting and regimenting his sexual behavior.

In this case, interpretations of the meaning of the concrete symbols were not effective in alleviating the sexual inhibitions. Increasingly, as the analysis progressed, the patient's associations drifted to his father, who crystallized in his memories as an elusive, uninvolved, emotionally absent figure, absorbed in a Walter Mittylike world of private fantasy and reverie, and offering little in the way of strength and protection to his son. It was only when in the transference the analyst became established as an emotionally present, involved paternal selfobject whom, unlike his father, the patient could experience as a powerful ally against the "insatiable" demands of the maternal imago, that the sexual inhibitions abated. As the patient felt the integrity of his individual selfhood sustained by the selfobject transference bond, the self-conserving concretizations became less necessary, thereby freeing his sexual life to become increasingly spontaneous and a source of pleasure for him.

SYMBOLIC OBJECTS

An important contribution to the understanding of the role of concretization in human psychological life was Winnicott's (1951) concept of the transitional object. He focused in particular on the small child's use of a soft object to master the anxiety and depressive affect evoked by early experiences of separation—both physical separation from the mother and the associated psychological differentiation of self from nonself, of subjective from objective reality. The transitional object stands for the breast-mother and creates an *illusion* of reunion with the missing maternal presence. In our terms, the material object symbolically encapsulates the soothing, comforting, calming qualities of the maternal selfobject, and the concretization serves a restitutive function in mending or replacing the broken merger.

Transitional objects are often used by patients to restore or maintain the bond with their therapist during separations. An interesting example of this occurred in the analysis of a 31-year-old man (whose treatment was described in Stolorow & Lachmann, 1980, chapter 7) who suffered from highly disturbing, foglike states of self-dissolution in reaction to injuries and rebuffs which, for him, disconfirmed his very existence. During a period of the treatment when he was in the process of establishing a stable selfobject transference relationship with the analyst, he made use of a tape recorder in a manner that proved to be highly therapeutic. In the wake of mortifications and disappointments, he would record his feelings on tape, and then listen to the recording with the same understanding attitude he had experienced from the therapist. This use of the tape recorder as a transitional object both concretized the injured state of the self and reinvoked the empathic bond with the therapist, thereby enabling the patient to regain a sense of being substantial and real.

Winnicott's conceptualization of the transitional object can, in our view, be seen as a particular instance of a more general psychological process whereby needed configurations of experience are symbolically materialized by means of concrete physical objects. Such concretizations can serve a restitutive function, but they can serve other psychological purposes as well, as further examples show.

A 35-year-old woman's crushing early history had left her with the feeling that she was absolutely worthless as a person and, in her essence, utterly repugnant to other human beings. Thus any attempt at a close relationship brought an almost unbearable sense of vulnerability and a terror of rejection which, for her, would confirm the conviction that her inner core was rotten and revolting to others. During the course of her psychotherapy she began to use symbolic objects in a particular way to counteract this extreme vulnerability and terror. At some point during the development of a friendship she would indicate to the person with whom she sought to be close that she wished to possess some object, usually an inexpensive trinket. If the prospective friend responded by buying that object for her, the patient would experience this as tangible evidence that the person found her worthy, and her feeling of vulnerability would subside markedly. If such friendships ended or failed to develop further, the patient would continue to cherish these gifts as concrete reminders of her having had value for other persons. Here the physical objects symbolically encapsulated a newly emerging quality of self-worth, and the concretizations served to consolidate and solidify this still unsteady and fragile aspect of her self-experience. She used symbolic objects to fortify various other therapeutic transformations in her sense of self as well. For example, she often punctuated the discovery or development of new aspects of herself by purchasing specific articles of clothing or decorative items for her home— objects that symbolically reified the new qualities of self.

In another young woman's early history, the mother's extreme self-absorption and inability to be genuinely interested in her children's needs had made it necessary for the patient to rely on her father as her primary caregiving figure. The father was able to provide caring and concern, but increasingly included his daughter in his own fearful, hypochondriacal view of himself. His hypochondriacal worrying extended specifically to her emotional life, so that he reacted to any strong needs or feelings in her, including loving ones, as if these were fatal flaws in her character, rendering her unfit for survival in and acceptance by the world. This had resulted in a painful division within herself, whereby deep aspects of her affective life had to be kept dissociated from her overt functioning with others.

As this aspect of her history and its impact were explored in the therapy, the analyst gradually became established in the transference as a selfobject whose acceptance and positive valuation of her needs and feelings were enabling her to reunite with ever-widening spheres of her emotionality. During this period she developed a strong, loving bond with a teddy bear, who provided her with warm, affectionate contact, and whom she cared for with great tenderness. It was a source of intense joy for her that she could be allowed these needs and feelings in relation to the teddy bear, as this seemed to embody her emerging hope of finding emotional fulfillment in the world. The patient indicated an awareness that the teddy bear enabled her to maintain the bond with her therapist when away from sessions, much as Winnicott described. More importantly, however, the relationship to the teddy bear served to concretize and consolidate her increasingly successful efforts to recover and reintegrate her "lost world of feelings" (Miller, 1979, p. 9) and to resume a process of emotional growth that had been derailed.

Interesting examples of the use of physical objects to sustain an endangered sense of self can be found in the psychological history of Carl Jung, during a critical period of his childhood between the ages of seven and ten. Upon entering school and becoming immersed in the society of schoolmates following an early childhood spent almost entirely alone, Jung felt his sense of identity to be extremely vulnerable and susceptible to powerful influences from his new social milieu. His attempts to protect against the danger of self-loss took the form of a set of secret, quasi-religious rituals involving a series of unique, symbolic objects—fires he tended and considered eternal, an immutable stone, and a small wooden maniken. These sacred objects and the corresponding rituals concretized his efforts to stabilize and fortify a precarious sense of integrity and individual selfhood by creating the illusion of an imperishable self existing in a sealed-off world of self-sufficiency and omnipotent splendor (an illusion to which his central metapsychological constructs later become heir; see Stolorow & Atwood, 1979, chapter 3, for a detailed analysis).

ENACTMENTS

The significance of enactment in concretizing and maintaining organizations of experience is implicit in our conceptualization of character as the structure of a subjective world (see chapter 1). This conceptualization assumes, in particular, that recurrent patterns of conduct serve to actualize (Sandler & Sandler, 1978) the nuclear configurations of self and object that constitute a person's character. Such patterns of conduct may include inducing others to act in predetermined ways, so that a thematic isomorphism is created between the ordering of the subjective and the interpersonal fields.

The proposition that the patterning of human conduct serves to maintain the organization of experience can be understood to apply in two senses. On the one hand, a pattern of conduct may serve to maintain a *particular* organization of experience, in which specific configurations of self and object, deriving from multiple origins and serving multiple purposes, are materialized. Such configurations, when actualized, may in varying degrees fulfill cherished wishes and urgent desires, provide moral restraint and self-punishment, aid adaptation to difficult realities, and repair or restore damaged or lost self and object images. They may also serve a defensive function in preventing other, subjectively dangerous configurations from emerging in conscious experience. Any or all of these aims can contribute to the formation of a pattern of conduct, and it is essential in psychoanalytic therapy to determine the relative motivational salience or priority of the purposes that a pattern of action serves.

On the other hand, a pattern of conduct may serve not so much to materialize a particular configuration of experience, but rather to maintain psychological organization per se, as when behavioral enactments are required to sustain the structural cohesion and continuity of a fragmenting sense of self or other. This most fundamental functional relationship between experience and conduct, whereby concrete courses of action are required to maintain the structural integrity and stability of the subjective world, we now illustrate through a consideration of sexual enactments.

The question arises: Why can some people actualize their psychological structures primarily in dreams, fantasies, personal myths, social role relationships, and other such systems of symbolization, while other people need to perform dramatic, often bizarre behavioral enactments to maintain their psychological organizations? In general, to the extent that severe developmental traumata, voids, and arrests have interfered with the structuralization of the subjective world, vivid concrete enactments tend to be required for restoring or maintaining vulnerable, disintegration-prone structures of experience (Stolorow & Lachmann, 1980). This formulation is crucial to the understanding and analytic approach to both overt destructiveness and sexual perversion. So-called sexual and aggressive "acting-out" is conceptualized not in terms of a defective "mental apparatus" lacking in "impulse control," but rather in terms of the person's need for behavioral enactments to shore up an imperiled subjective world.

A second question arises: Why do many people use *sexual* enactments for this purpose of restoring or maintaining precarious structures of subjectivity? Some answers to this question can be found by examining the contribution of early psychosexual experiences to the development of the subjective world and to the structuralization of the sense of self in particular, and also by considering a special quality of the experience of sexual pleasure with respect to the affirmation of truth and conviction.

With regard to the role of sensual experiences in articulating the developing child's subjective world, a number of authors (e.g., Hoffer, 1950; Mahler et al. 1975) have suggested that the delineation of a rudimentary body image is accomplished through the sensual stimulations of the child's body surface resulting from pleasureable contacts within the mother-infant interactions. More specifically, the epigenetic unfolding of psychosexual modes, as described by Erikson (1950), can be shown to serve in critical ways the consolidation of a sense of an individualized self differentiated from primary objects (Stolorow, 1979; Stolorow & Lachmann, 1980).

Experiences and fantasies in the oral-incorporative mode contribute to the process of self-object differentiation by concretizing the subjective distinction between inside and outside, between the self as a container and the nonself which can be taken in. At the same time, the child may employ incorporative fantasies to symbolize the appropriation of valued and admired qualities of objects to his own sense of self, contributing further to its structuralization.

Experiences and fantasies in the anal-retentive mode provide concrete symbols for a stubborn affirmation of the boundaries separating self and nonself, a definitive milestone in self-object differentiation. Through anal-eliminative acts and fantasies, the child symbolically ejects undesirable contents from his sense of self, further promoting its individualization and refining its demarcation from the object world.

A decisive step in self-definition occurs with the discovery of genital differences and the unfolding of the intrusive and inclusive genital modes, which begin to distinguish the sensual self-experience of boys and girls respectively. As with oral-incorporative and anal-aggressive fantasies, phallic imagery too can serve to buttress the vulnerable sense of self of developing children of both sexes. The oedipal saga itself may be viewed as a pivotal phase in the structuralization of the self (Kohut, 1977), which finds its unique form in emerging from the conflictual flux of experiences of phallic grandeur and depletion, rivalrous triumph and defeat, threats to genital intactness, and envy of the penis or womb.

Thus we see that nature, in her evolutionary wisdom, has harnassed the exquisiteness of sensual pleasure to serve the ontogenesis of human subjectivity. The sensual experiences and fantasies that occur in the course of early development may be viewed as psychic organizers that contribute vitally to the structuralization of the subjective world and of the sense of self in particular. Psychosexual experiences provide the child with an array of sensorimotor and anatomical symbols that serve to concretize and solidify developmental steps in the articulation of his subjective universe. When these developments are seriously impeded, leading to structural deficits and weaknesses, the person may as an adult continue to look to psychosexual symbols to maintain the organization of his subjective life. By dramatically enacting these concrete symbolic forms to the accompaniment of orgasm, he gives vividly reified, tangible substance to his efforts to restore a failing sense of self. In such instances of sexual perversion, it is not, contrary to what Freud (1905) maintained, the infantile erotic experience per se that has been fixated and then regressively reanimated. Instead, it is the early *function* of the erotic experience that is retained and regressively relied upon— its function in maintaining the cohesion and stability of a sense of self menaced with disintegration. Analytic exploration of the details of perverse enactments, their origins and functions, should reveal the particular ways in which they both encapsulate the danger to the self and embody a concretizing effort at self-restoration.

A number of analysts have contributed important insights into the function of perserve activity in shoring up precarious structures of experience. Socarides (1978), for example, has shown how homosexual patterns can protect against the danger of self-object boundary dissolution. The function of sexual activity in restoring or maintaining a fragile sense of self has been explored in detail by Kohut (1971, 1977) and Goldberg (1975). They have found that a wide variety of perverse activities may be viewed as sexualized attempts to compensate for voids and defects in the sense of self and to counteract experiences of inner deadness and self-fragmentation. In the perverse enactment, the person sexualizes a fragment of an archaic narcissistic configuration in an effort to find an eroticized replacement for the selfobjects who in his formative years were traumatically absent, disappointing, or unresponsive to his developmental requirements.

In previous work (Stolorow & Lachmann, 1980), an attempt was made to develop some of these notions further by examining the functions of masochistic perversion. It was suggested that in persons with deficits in psychological structure formation, masochistic experiences can serve to restore or sustain a damaged, menaced, or disintegrating sense of self through the stimulations afforded by pain and skin eroticism, through exhibitionistic displays of suffering to a real or imagined audience, through mergings with omnipotent object images, and by actualizing an archaic grandiose self. Extrapolating from the ideas of Nydes (1950) and Eissler (1958) on the power of sexual pleasure and of orgasm to create and affirm conviction, it was proposed that the experience of orgasm in sadomasochistic perversions serves to revitalize ecstatically the person's sense of conviction about the truth and reality of his having a bounded and cohesive self. The Janus-faced quality of the orgasm, it was further suggested, in both offering the promise of self-articulation and posing the threat of self-dissolution, accounts for the elaborate ritualization often surrounding perverse enactments.

An illustration of the function of perverse enactments in repairing and sustaining an insufficiently structured sense of self is provided by the case of Mark[1], a young man who sought treatment, not for his homosexuality, but for the disturbances in self-esteem triggered by disappointments in the pace of his professional advancement. Analytic reconstructions traced the origins of the vulnerability in his self-esteem to his early tie to his mother, a vain, self-engrossed woman who possessed little ability to provide Mark with either the warm, sensual body contact or the confirmations that are prerequisites for the rudimentary consolidation of a cohesive and stable self-structure. As a child, he had maintained a precarious grandiose self-organization by embracing the role of mother's confidant, her "little gentleman" and self-extension. At the same time, his mother undermined his more independent grandiose and phallic-exhibitionistic strivings, frequently subjecting him to ridicule and severe shamings, drastically interfering with the consolidation of his sense of self. This history of repeated mortification had become encapsulated and

---

[1]This clinical illustration was originally provided by Dr. Frank M. Lachmann and is described in greater detail in Stolorow & Lachmann, 1980, chapter 8.

concretized in early memories of searing humiliation when he "embarassed" his mother by urinating on the floor.

Associations to these early traumatic shame experiences disclosed three phases in the development of Mark's homosexuality, shedding light on its function in sustaining his sense of self. During his early teen years he would periodically urinate on the kitchen floor in order to roll around on his urine. This enactment was understood in terms of his need to shore up the intactness of his precarious self-boundaries by transforming a symbolic encapsulation of narcissistic trauma—his urine—into a replacement for the warm, sensual, confirming contact that his mother had failed to provide. Somewhat later in his adolescence, self-restoration by rolling in his urine was replaced by masturbation in front of a mirror in which he imagined the sight of a perfect version of himself, whereupon he could feel for the moment transformed into an imaginary picture of physical perfection. The self-reparative and self-restitutive functions of these earlier practices acquired a definitive, enduring sexualization in the homosexuality that germinated during his later college years. Two essential components in his homosexual experiences were, first, that they were enacted exhibitionistically, in a public homosexual setting where he could feel enhanced by the admiration of his onlookers, and second, that they made possible a union with an admiring, idealized, sexually identical partner who simultaneously confirmed and duplicated Mark's own archaic, wishfully perfect, grandiose self. In their mirror-functions, his audience and his partner were heirs to the urine and to the literal mirror of his earlier pubertal years. The exhibitionistic homosexual enactments provided his sense of self with a modicum of cohesion and stability by actualizing an archaic illusion of perfection, stamped by the sexual orgasm with a feeling of conviction and reality.

To summarize, we have considered sexual perversion to be an example of the most fundamental functional relationship between experience and conduct, whereby concrete courses of action are required for maintaining the structural integrity of a subjective world. We have suggested that sexual enactments are especially well suited to serve this purpose because of the developmental importance of concrete psychosexual symbols in the

articulation of a child's experience, and because of the special capacity of sexual pleasure and orgasm to create and affirm conviction. And finally, we have proposed that sexual enactments occuring in the context of structural deficits, as was the case with
Mark, can be shown both to encapsulate the danger to the self and
to embody a concretizing effort at self-restoration. Such enactments thus provide a dramatic example of the role of
concretization in maintaining the organization of experience.

Seen from an intersubjective perspective, the therapeutic implications of viewing sexual perversions as concretized symbolic
residues of developmental deficits in psychological structure formation are profound. The patient must be permitted to revive
with the therapist the archaic mirroring, idealizing, and other
selfobject ties on which the early development of his subjective
life had foundered and through which this development can be
once again resumed. Ordinarily, once the selfobject transference
relationship becomes reliably established, it tends to absorb the
functions previously served by the perversion in maintaining the
intactness of the patient's self-experience. Hence the perverse activity tends to recede and even disappear, only to return, intensify, or assume a more primitive form when the selfobject transference bond becomes significantly ruptured by empathic failures
or separations (Kohut, 1971). Perverse activities—indeed, all
products of the concretization process—cannot be comprehended
apart from the intersubjective contexts in which they arise and
recede. The understanding of the meaning of perverse enactments, in particular their functions in shoring up an endangered
sense of self in the context of a disrupted selfobject tie, can be pivotal to the analysis and working through of the transference, and
hence to the formation and consolidation of new structures of experience.

DREAMS

Historically, the psychoanalytic concept of the unconscious
evolved in concert with the interpretation of dreams (Freud,
1900). A significant expansion of the concept of the unconscious

should therefore hold important implications for the psychoanalytic approach to dreams. It is our contention that an understanding of the form of unconsciousness that we have designated as "prereflective" sheds new light on the unique importance of dreams for psychoanalytic theory and practice. The prereflective structures of a person's subjective world are most readily discernible in his relatively unfettered, spontaneous productions, and there is probably no psychological product that is less fettered or more spontaneous than the dream. As human subjectivity in purest culture, the dream constitutes a "royal road" to the prereflective unconscious—to the organizing principles and dominant leitmotivs that unconsciously pattern and thematize a person's psychological life.[2] In the remainder of this chapter, we explore some clinical and theoretical implications of this close proximity of the dream to the unconscious structures of experience. We offer first some general remarks on the nature of psychoanalytic dream interpretation.

The Nature of Dream Interpretation

In classical psychoanalysis, the technical procedure for arriving at the meaning of a dream is to decompose the dream into discrete elements and then to collect the dreamer's associations to each of these elements. The rationale for this procedure is found in the theoretical idea that the associative chains provided by the dreamer, supplemented by certain connections and additions suggested by the analyst, will retrace the mental processes that gave rise to the dream and will lead the way back to the dream's latent content or unconscious meaning. It is assumed that the meaning of a dream, as determined by this method, is identical to the dream's causal origin; that is, the latent thoughts and wishes disclosed by the analysis are regarded as having been the elemental starting points of the dream's formation.

From the perspective of a framework that takes human subjectivity as its central focus, the determination of the meaning of a

---

[2]From a different theoretical perspective, Erikson (1954) has suggested that attention to the dream's "style of representation" can reveal the dreamer's modes of experiencing himself and his world.

dream is a matter of elucidating the ways in which the dream is embedded in the ongoing course of the dreamer's experiencing. By restoring dream symbols and metaphors to their formative personal contexts, interpretation rebuilds the links between dream imagery and the salient concerns of the dreamer's subjective life. In developing a phenomenological approach to the psychology of dreams, we seek understanding of how dreams encapsulate the personal world and history of the dreamer. The utility of collecting free associations, from our standpoint, is thus not to retrace the presumed causal pathways of dream formation, but rather to *generate contexts of subjective meaning* in terms of which the dream imagery may be examined and understood. In addition to the discrete elements of a manifest dream, the distinctive thematic configurations of self and object that structure the dream narrative may also serve as useful points of departure for associative elaboration (Stolorow, 1978). Such themes, when abstracted from the concrete details of the dream and presented to the dreamer, can substantially enrich the associations that are produced and represent an important source of insight into the prereflectively unconscious structures of experience which organize a person's subjective world.

At the heart of the conceptual framework of psychoanalytic phenomenology is a set of interpretive principles for elucidating psychological phenomena in their personal contexts. With regard to dreams, these principles provide ways of viewing dream imagery against the background of the dreamer's subjective universe. Many such interpretive principles are implicit in the classical Freudian theory of how dreams are formed. We believe this theory is most profitably viewed as a hermeneutic system of rules of interpretation rather than as a causal-mechanistic account of the processes of dream generation. Freud (1900) argued that interpretation reverses the dream work—that the activity of dream analysis moves backward along the paths of dream formation. It would be more accurate to say that the *theory* of the dream work reverses the pathways followed by psychoanalytic interpretation. The dream-work "mechanism" of condensation, for example, is the theoretical reverse of the interpretive principle that a single element in the dream text may be related to a multiplicity of subjective contexts in the dreamer's psychological life. Similarly, the mechanism of displacement inverts the principle that one may transpose and interchange the affective accents on various elements in the dream narrative in order to identify subjectively dangerous or conflictual configurations of images that the dreamer may be attempting to prevent from crystallizing in awareness.

The classical notion that dreams represent (attempted) wish fulfillments can also be viewed as an interpretive principle guiding the quest for a dream's connection to the subjective concerns of the dreamer. By giving the analyst an initial bearing in confronting the complexity of a particular dream narrative, this premise provides an orienting focus in relating the dream to emotionally significant issues in the dreamer's life. We would expand the classical conception of the centrality of wish fulfillment in dreams into a more general and inclusive proposition that dreams always embody one or more of the dreamer's *personal purposes*. Such purposes include the fulfillment of wishes as discussed by Freud, but also a number of other important psychological purposes (self-guiding and self-punishing, adaptive, restitutive-reparative, defensive) as well. Any or all such personal motivations can contribute to the construction of a dream, and it is essential to the therapeutic use of dream interpretation to determine the relative motivational salience or priority of the multiple purposes that the dream has served.

The interpretive principles of psychoanalytic phenomenology as applied to dreams operate as aids to the interpreter in approaching the content of a manifest dream and its associations. They enable the analyst to construct a complex map of the various lines of symbolic expression which connect a dream to the personal world of the dreamer. The utility of these principles for examining a particular dream lies in the degree to which they lead to an interpretation that convincingly illuminates the various features of the dream text as embodiments of the issues and concerns having salience in the dreamer's subjective life. The correctness or adequacy of a particular dream interpretation, in turn, is assessed by the same hermeneutic criteria that govern the assessment of the validity of psychoanalytic interpretation in general (see chapter 1)—the logical coherence of the argument, the compatibility of the interpretation with one's general knowledge of the dreamer's psychological life, the comprehensiveness of the explanation in rendering the various details of the dream text transparent, and the aesthetic beauty of the analysis in illuminating previously hidden patterns of order in the dream narrative and in connecting these patterns to the background structures of the dreamer's personal subjectivity.

Let us now return from this general discussion of dream interpretation to a consideration of the central attribute of the dream experience—concrete symbolization.

Concrete Symbolization in Dreams

Among recent critiques of Freudian theory, some of the most constructive have been those that rest upon George Klein's (1976) clarifying distinction between the metapsychology and the clinical theory of psychoanalysis. Metapsychology and clinical theory, Klein held, derive from two completely different universes of discourse. Metapsychology deals with the presumed material substrate of human experience, and is thus couched in the natural science framework of impersonal mechanisms, discharge apparatuses, and drive energies. In contrast, clinical theory, which derives from the psychoanalytic situation and guides psychoanalytic practice, deals with intentionality, conscious and unconscious purposes, and the personal meaning of subjective experiences. Klein wished to disentangle metapsychological and clinical concepts, and to retain only the latter as the legitimate content of psychoanalytic theory.

In this section we first comment briefly on Freud's two theories of the dream work—the metapsychological and the clinical. We then offer a clinical psychoanalytic theory of the purpose of concrete symbolization in dreams, based on the framework of psychoanalytic phenomenology.

Freud's metapsychological theory of the dream work finds its clearest expression in Chapter 7 of *The Interpretation of Dreams* (1900). There the dream work (with the exception of secondary revision) is conceptualized as a nonpurposeful, mechanical consequence of a process whereby preconscious thoughts receive an energic charge from an unconscious wish "striving to find an outlet" (p. 605). The dream work occurs as the preconscious thoughts are "drawn into the unconscious" (p. 594) and thereby automatically "become subject to the primary psychical process" (p. 603).

In contrast with this mechanistic view of the dream work, germs of a clinical theory emphasizing its intentional and purposeful quality appear in an earlier chapter on "Distortion in Dreams." There the dream work is seen "to be deliberate and to be a means of dissimulation" (p. 141) and disguise, serving the purpose of defense. In these passages, we can readily recognize the dream censor as being the dreamer himself, actively transforming the content and meaning of his experiences in order to protect himself from direct awareness of forbidden wishes.

This germinal clinical theory of the dream work, emphasizing its defensive purpose, applies principally to the process of displacement, and perhaps also to condensation. It does not shed a great deal of light on what we regard as the most distinctive and central feature of the dream experience—the use of concrete perceptual images endowed with hallucinatory vividness to symbolize abstract thoughts, feelings, and subjective states. Freud's explanation of this feature of dreams was an entirely metapsychological one: A "topographical regression" (p. 548) of excitation from the motor to the sensory end of the psychic apparatus was thought to result in "a hallucinatory revival of . . . perceptual images" (p. 543). Thus, in Freud's view, the pictorial and hallucinatory quality of dreams was a nonpurposeful, mechanical consequence of the discharge path followed by psychic energy during sleep. In contrast, we are proposing that concrete symbolization in dreams and their resulting hallucinatory vividness serve a vital psychological purpose for the dreamer, and that an understanding of this purpose can illuminate the importance and necessity of dreaming.

It is in the need to maintain the organization of experience, our supraordinate motivational principle, that we can discover the fundamental purpose of concrete symbolization in dreams. When configurations of experience of self and other find symbolization in concrete perceptual images and are thereby articulated with hallucinatory vividness, the dreamer's feeling of conviction about the validity and reality of these configurations receives a powerful reinforcement. Perceiving, after all, is believing. By reviving during sleep the most basic and emotionally compelling form of knowing—through sensory perception—the dream affirms and solidifies the nuclear organizing structures of the dreamer's subjective life. Dreams, we are contending, are the *guardians of psychological structure,* and they fulfill this vital purpose by means of concrete symbolization.[3]

Closely paralleling the two senses in which patterns of conduct function to sustain structures of subjectivity, the claim that dream symbolization serves to maintain the organization of experience can be seen to apply in two different senses to two broad classes of dreams (with many dreams, of course, combining features of both classes). In some dreams, concrete symbols serve to actualize a *particular* organization of experience in which specific configurations of self and object, required for multiple reasons, are dramatized and affirmed. Dreams of this first class appear most often in the context of firmly structured emotional conflict. With these dreams there is usually a wide gap between their manifest imagery and latent meaning, because the aims of defense and disguise have been prominent in their construction. Our approach to such dreams incorporates what we earlier referred to as Freud's clinical theory of the dream work, particularly as this was later updated to include the principle of multiple function (Waelder, 1936; Arlow & Brenner, 1964). As we discussed in the preceding section, we also supplement the classical approach with a focus on dream themes and their associative elaboration, as a further means of discovering the specific configurations of self and object that the dream symbolism has both actualized and disguised.

---

[3]Lerner (1967) has presented evidence that dreams, through their kinesthetic elements, function to strengthen the body image. This, if true, would be a special, circumscribed instance of the broader thesis we are proposing here. Formulations of the problem-solving (Freud, 1900), focal conflict-resolving (French & Fromm, 1964), and trauma-integrating (de Monchaux, 1978) functions of dreams may also be seen as special instances of the role of dream symbolization in maintaining the organization of experience. Fosshage (1983) has arrived independently at a formulation similar to ours.

In another class of dreams, concrete symbols serve not so much to actualize particular configurations of experience, but rather to maintain psychological organization per se. Dreams of this second class occur most often in the context of developmental interferences and arrests, whereby structuralization of the subjective world has remained incomplete, precarious, and vulnerable to dissolution. With these dreams the distinction between manifest and latent content is much less germane, because the aim of disguise has not been prominent. Instead, the vivid perceptual images of the dream serve directly to restore or sustain the structural integrity and stability of a subjective world menaced with disintegration. We have seen that for persons with severe deficits in psychological structure formation, concretization may serve a similar purpose in their waking lives as well, not only in the form of delusions and hallucinations, but also in the concrete behavioral enactments, often of a destructive or sexual nature, that are required to sustain the cohesion and continuity of a fragmenting sense of self or other.

An important subgroup of this second class of dreams, in which concrete symbols serve to maintain psychological organization per se, are the "self-state dreams" discussed by Kohut (1977). These dreams portray in their manifest imagery "the dreamer's dread vis-a-vis some uncontrollable tension-increase or his dread of the dissolution of the self" (p. 109). Kohut suggests that the very act of portraying these archaic self-states in the dream in a minimally disguised form "constitutes an attempt to deal with the psychological danger by covering frightening nameless processes with namable visual imagery" (p. 109). Socarides (1980) has discovered a similar purpose fulfilled by dreams that directly depict perverse sexual enactments similar to those performed by the dreamer in his waking life. The hallucinatory visualization of the perversion during sleep, like the perverse enactment itself, shores up an imperiled sense of self and protects against the danger of its dissolution.

The principal purpose of the perceptual imagery of self-state dreams is not, in our view, to render nameless psychological processes namable. By vividly reifying the experience of self-endangerment, the dream symbols bring the state of the self into focal awareness with a feeling of conviction and reality that can only accompany sensory perceptions. The dream images, like sexual enactments, both encapsulate the danger to the self and reflect a concretizing effort at self-restoration. Thus, self-state dreams too represent an instance of our general thesis concerning the central role of concretization in maintaining the organization of experience.

Clinical Illustration[4]

The case we have chosen to illustrate our conception of the structure-maintaining function of concrete symbolization in dreams is that of a young woman whose sense of self had become fragmented into a set of separate, quasi-autonomous personalities. The dreams discussed reflect various aspects of her lifelong struggle to maintain the organization of her subjective world and achieve unity and cohesion in her self-experience. A feature of this case making it especially well suited for this discussion is that the patient engaged in specific concrete behavioral enactments which served a purpose closely paralleling that of her dreams. Viewing her dreams in the context of these enactments will bring the organization-maintaining function of her dream imagery into sharp focus.

The family environment in which the patient grew up was one of extreme physical and emotional abuse. Both parents treated her as an extension of themselves and as a scapegoat for their frustrations and disappointments in life. Violent physical beatings represented a frequent form of interaction with the parents, and throughout her early childhood she thought they wished her dead. A sense of profound personal disunity had haunted the patient all her life, appearing even in her earliest recollections. For example, she recalled from her fourth year an obsession with the issue of how it could be that her mind controlled the movements

[4]Since dreams of the first type, in which the perceptual images serve to actualize a particular organization of experience required for multiple reasons, are very familiar to analysts, they will not be exemplified here. We will illustrate only dreams of the second type, in which the imagery serves principally to maintain psychological organization per se.

of her body. A disturbance in mind-body unity was also indicated by quasi-delusional journeys outside of her body, which began during that same year. These journeys commenced on the occasion when she was visited by the benevolent ghosts of two deceased grandparents. The ghosts taught her to leave her body and fly to a place she called "the field," a peaceful expanse of grass and trees somewhere far removed from human society. She felt safe in the field because she was alone there and no one could find her.

The psychological disintegration implicit in the patient's out-of-the-body journeys was embedded in a broader context of self-division resulting from the violent abuse and rejection she had received in her family. Beginning at the age of two and one-half, when her parents abruptly ceased all affectionate bodily contact with her, and continuing through a series of pivotal traumatic episodes over the next several years, she was successively divided into a total of six fragmentary selves. Each of these fragments crystallized as a distinct personality, possessing its own individual name and unique personal attributes.

When the patient was seven years old she developed a renal tumor, causing agonizing pain. The need to escape the suffering generated by her condition became an additional motive underlying the journeys outside of her body. It was more than one full year before her illness was correctly diagnosed and the tumor finally removed. The surgery itself was handled with brutal insensitivity by her parents and doctors, and she experienced it as an overwhelming trauma. The impact of all these circumstances on her precarious selfhood was symbolized in a set of recurring nightmares that began during her recuperation from surgery and continued throughout her life thereafter. In these dreams she stood alone in the small train station of her town as flames sprang up all around her. Soon the whole building was engulfed in fire. After the station had burned to the ground, two eyeballs lay quietly in the smoking ashes and then began to quiver and roll about, conversing with each other by means of movements and glances. This dream of burning down to small fragments concretely depicted the disintegrating impact of a world persecuting her both from without and from within.

What psychological function can be ascribed to the patient's recurring dream of being burned down to isolated fragments? The repeated transformation of the experience of self-disintegration into an image of the physical incineration of her body enabled her to maintain the state of her self in focal awareness and encapsulated her effort to retain psychological integrity in the face of the threat of total self-dissolution. By utilizing concrete anatomical imagery, she was giving her disintegrating existence tangible form, replacing a precarious and vanishing sense of selfhood with the permanence and substantiality of physical matter. The image of the interaction and communication between the eyeballs at the end of the dream symbolized a further restitutive effort to reconnect the broken fragments and restore a measure of coherence to her splintered self. The specific symbol of the eyeballs captured an essential feature of what became her principal mode of relating to her social milieu. She assumed the role of an ever-watchful, often disembodied spectator, perpetually scanning her environment for desirable qualities in others that she hoped to appropriate and assemble into a rebuilt self. Thus, both her self-restorative efforts and what remained of her vanishing self became crystallized in her waking life in the act of looking and in her recurring dreams in the imagery of the eyes.

The central salience in the patient's subjective world of the need to maintain selfhood and recover a sense of personal unity was also indicated by an array of bizarre enactments that appeared concurrently with the onset of the recurring dream of being burned. These enactments included the self-administration of severe whippings with a leather belt, delicate cutting and puncturing of the surface of the skin on her wrists and arms, gazing tirelessly at the reflected image of her face in pools of water, fondling and staring into translucent pieces of glass, scratching and rubbing at cracks and crevices in hard physical surfaces such as walls and sidewalks, and stitching the skin of her separate fingers together with needle and thread. Since the appearance of the enactments coincided precisely with the onset of the recurrent nightmare, we have regarded the enactments as "associations" embedded in the same contexts of meaning in which the dream imagery took form.

The self-whipping ritual arose initially as an internalization of the punishing treatment the patient had received during her earlier childhood. She tended at first to whip herself in response to acts that previously would have evoked her parents' wrath—e.g., acts of asserting her needs, seeking attention, or expressing unhappiness. The function of the self-punishments at this stage was primarily to master a sense of helplessness and counteract the dreaded feeling of being vulnerable to attack from the outside world. The ritual also came to include a wish-fulfilling and restitutive element in the form of a sequel to the actual whipping. After first violently beating herself on the back and buttocks, she would adopt the role of loving parent and say to herself in a soft voice, "It's all right honey, now there will be no more pain." Then assuming the role of comforted child, she would fall blissfully asleep. This hard-won feeling of peacefulness, however, was rudely shattered when she later awoke and found herself still entirely alone.

In addition to helping her master persecution anxiety and maintain needed images of herself being cared for by good objects, the whipping ritual also began to serve a more fundamental purpose in the patient's subjective life. One of the consequences of her profound and enduring emotional isolation was a feeling of being unreal, unalive, and insubstantial. This feeling was magnified by the continuing out-of-the-body journeys to the field. The increasing frequency of these journeys came to pose a new and even more menacing danger to her safety—namely, the severing of all connection to physical reality and the final obliteration of her psychic self. The terror that she might permanently lose her physical form and somehow evaporate into thin air led her to return to the whipping ritual with redoubled intensity. The strong sensations of pain distributed on the surface of her skin were used to provide reassurance of her continuing embodiment and survival in the real physical world.

Essentially parallel functions were served by the patient's ritualistic cutting and puncturing of the skin on her wrists and arms. These behaviors seemed to originate as a restaging of the traumatically impinging medical procedures associated with her renal surgery. In addition to the operation itself, the procedures included a spinal tap, numerous injections, catheterization, intravenous administration of medications and fluids, etc. By cutting and puncturing her skin, she actively relived a passively endured trauma and sought mastery over her feelings of unbearable helplessness. Like the ritualized whipping, the cutting and puncturing activity also began to serve the function of strengthening the patient's conviction that she was substantial and real. By violating the physical boundary of her body with a needle or a knife, she dramatized the very existence of that boundary and reestablished a sense of her own embodied selfhood. In addition, the stinging sensations and the droplets of blood produced by the delicate cutting provided her with concrete sensory evidence of her continuing aliveness.

The enactments involving water and glass were more complex, but also related to struggles with a precarious self-structure and a deep sense of helpless vulnerability. The water ritual began when she gazed at her reflection in ponds and pools of rainwater. She recalled becoming fascinated by how the image of her face would disappear and then magically reappear when she disturbed the water's reflecting surface. One meaning of this activity pertained again to her need for mastery over passively experienced traumata—by actively being the cause of the disappearance of her image she was seeking to overcome the shattering impact on her sense of selfhood of her whole earlier history of victimization and abuse. In addition, in eliminating her reflected image she thought of herself as actually ceasing to exist and becoming nothing, which provided a feeling of safety because what does not exist cannot be made a target by a persecuting world. The water also seemed to function as a transitional selfobject, giving reassurance that while her sense of self (concretized in a visual reflection) might be made to vanish on a temporary basis, it could not be annihilated permanently. A sense of self-continuity was thus tenuously achieved. A final significance of water to the patient was associated with its paradoxical quality of being both *transparent* and *reflecting*. There was something in the conjoining of these two properties with which she wishfully identified, and this identification was even more pronounced in her involvement with objects of glass.

The patient began to collect small glass objects during her early adolescence. The reflecting and refracting properties of crystal prisms and spheres particularly fascinated her. Acts of fondling and staring into such objects developed into a ritual behavior pattern duplicating and sometimes blending into her relationship with water. On occasion she would fill a crystal container with water and place it in a window where she could observe its interaction with the sun's rays. This ritual was enacted several times during the psychotherapeutic sessions. As she studied the interplay between the light, the water, and the glass, she would softly chant, "water . . . glass . . . water . . . glass." Her consciousness could become wholly absorbed in this preoccupation, which she seemed to experience as a refuge from the social environment. The psychological sources of the patient's attraction to glass were bound up with her difficulties in maintaining a feeling of her own personal selfhood. She was excessively vulnerable to the expectations and perceptions of others, and tended to feel that she became whomever she was seen as being. For instance, when a grandfather told her wistfully how much she reminded him of his long-dead beloved wife, the patient felt the departed soul of the wife invading and assuming command over her body. Such episodes drastically affected her sense of being in possession of her own identity, and she responded to them by cultivating secret realms of herself protected from the annihilating potential of others' perceptions and definitions. Included in the elaboration of these hidden sectors of her subjective life was the development of her alternative personalities, each christened with its own secret name. The fact that no one knew her secret names made her feel safe from the engulfing potential of others' experiences of her. A consequence of the patient's defensive secrecy, however, was a further intensification of her feeings of estrangement. She was driven into isolation in order to protect herself from self-loss in relationships; but the isolation itself presented the danger of self-extinction through unendurable loneliness. Her preoccupation with glass sprang directly from the conflict between her need to retreat from others into a world of secrecy and her need to break out of isolation and reestablish bonds to the social environment. The glass concretized a wishful solution to this conflict by embodying the twin properties of translucency on the one hand and reflectivity on the other. The translucency of the glass meant that it was open to the passage of light from the outside, which served to lessen the patient's fear of isolation and entombment within her own secret world. The reflectivity of the glass objects, their solidity, and their firm boundaries, by contrast, meant that they were real and substantial, which made her feel safe from the dangers posed by involvement with her social milieu. A fusion of these properties also appeared in a recurring fantasy concerning a house she wished to build in the field she had been visiting in the out-of-the-body projections. She pictured this house as a beautiful construction of one-way glass, so that from the outside it would be a mirror, but from the inside transparent.

The remaining enactments to be considered were those in which the patient scratched and rubbed at cracks in solid surfaces and stitched her fingers together with thread. These enactments pertained to the patient's experience of being an assembly of disjointed parts. With regard to the scratching pattern, she explained that crevices and cracks in the external environment "itched" unbearably and compelled her to scratch them. The locating of the subjective sensation of itching in physical objects represented a transposition onto the plane of material reality of her feeling of inner fragmentation. She described herself as being like a jar filled with small spheres or cubes with concave surfaces, and as a checkerboard filled with round checkers; even though the constituent elements might be packed together very tightly, they still would not form an integrated and smoothly continuous whole. The itching cracks and crevices in the external environment corresponded to the subjective interstices between the various fragmentary entities comprising her self-experience, and the scratching represented her effort to find relief from her distressing lack of inner cohesion.

Closely similar was the function of her pattern of sewing her fingers together with needle and thread. This ritual began with holding her hand up to the light and gazing at the spaces between her separate fingers. Then she would push a needle and thread just under the skin of her little finger, then under the skin of the next one, and the next, etc., and then back and forth several times until they were all tightly interconnected and pressed together. The act of weaving the fingers together was one in which separate parts of her physical self were literally joined and made to appear whole and continuous, concretizing her effort to fashion an internally integrated identity out of the collection of part-selves into which she had divided during the course of her traumatic early history.

The enactments in which the patient engaged are functionally parallel to her recurring dreams of being burned to fragments. The essential feature the two sets of phenomena share in common is the reparative use of concretization to give an experience of self-disintegration a material and substantial form. In the dreams the emphasis appears on the concrete symbolization of the experience of self-dissolution, and the additional reparative trend of reassembling the broken pieces is hinted at in the image of the communication that develops between the eyeballs. In the enactments one finds analogous symbolizations and also the vivid expression of the patient's need to mend her broken self by reconnecting the separate fragments into which she had disintegrated.

Each of the patterns of behavior discussed here was repeatedly enacted during the psychotherapeutic sessions. Some of these performances were extremely difficult for the therapist to witness, especially those in which she slapped, whipped, and cut herself. For the first year and a half of treatment she brought knives, needles, pieces of broken glass, and a leather belt to the sessions on a regular basis and frequently used one or more of these objects against herself. When the therapist attempted to prevent this behavior by taking her objects away, she would scratch, slap, and beat herself with her hands and fingernails. The only means of ensuring that the patient would not engage in self-abuse was to physically restrain her until the self-destructive urges had passed. This physical restraining occupied a significant portion of many sessions during the early phases of the psychotherapeutic work and proved to be critically important in solidifying the therapeutic bond. In addition to the restraint required to prevent the patient from harming herself, there were a number of times when she approached her therapist and grasped him tightly, pressing her face against his body. After the first occasion of such an approach she explained she had needed the physical contact to prove he was not an unreal apparition or hallucination she had conjured up. She reported having been shocked and surprised when her arms met the solid resistance of his flesh, for she had expected them to pass right through him as though he were made of mist. Contact with her therapist's physical being served to differentiate him from the ghosts and other imaginary entities on whom she had previously depended. This contact also provided an anchoring point for the beginning stabilization of her own physical embodiment. It emerged in discussions of the meaning and significance of holding and being held that the patient had not experienced affectionate bodily contact with another human being since the age of two and one-half, when her parents ended all such interaction with her.

The first year and a half of the patient's treatment were devoted primarily to establishing a therapeutic relationship that would give her some relief from her estrangement and loneliness while at the same time strengthening her sense of individuality and separateness as a person. She oscillated during this period between expressions of suicidal despair and a mergerlike closeness in which she seemed to want nothing but physical proximity to the therapist. The actual physical contact, together with the symbolic holding (Winnicott, 1965) implicit in the therapist's consistent provision of acceptance, concern, and understanding, established a nexus of archaic relatedness in which the patient's aborted psychological development could move forward once again. Very gradually the functions inhering in the enactments we have described passed over to the empathic bond that was becoming established. The nature of the patient's evolving reliance on her analyst at the beginning of this process was shown by her reactions to his periodic failures to comprehend or appropriately respond to what she tried to communicate. Such misunderstandings tended to be followed by a resurgence of one or more of the enactments, which then continued until the disrupted empathic bond could be reestablished. As she increasingly came to rely on the therapist as a selfobject for the maintenance of her psychological organization, the ritualized enactments (and the out-of-the-body projections), which she had formerly needed for this purpose, lessened and finally disappeared. The repeating nightmares of being burned to fragments came to an end simultaneously.

The function of dreams in maintaining the organization of a person's subjective world is to be seen not only in situations wherein structures are breaking down, as was the case with the patient at the time of the onset of her nightmares; dreams may also play an important role in consolidating and stabilizing new structures of subjectivity which are in the process of coming into being. Let us turn now to a consideration of another dream of the patient we have been discussing, this one having occurred midway through the long course of her psychotherapy. The context of this dream in the treatment was one of intense conflict and struggle over the issue of self-unification. Two of the initial six part-selves had at this point been assimilated into the remaining four, but the next steps of integration were being approached by the patient with trepidation and reluctance. Specifically, she feared that becoming one would render her vulnerable to being destroyed, either by attack from the outside world or by unendurable loneliness. At the same time, however, she had come to abhor the prospect of a life spent in continuing disunity.

In her dream she walked into the living room of her house and saw on the mantle above the fireplace four cement boxes resting side by side. There seemed to be bodies inside the boxes. The scene terrified her and she awoke, but then fell back asleep and the dream continued. Now the four boxes were replaced by just one box, with four bodies arranged inside with their backs against the cement walls and facing inward toward a central point. The box seemed to be a coffin. In discussing this dream with the therapist, the patient spontaneously associated the four boxes with the four remaining part-selves still requiring integration. A great deal of progress toward this goal had already been achieved, principally through the four parts growing less and less distinct from each other in the facilitating medium of the therapeutic relationship. The patient was oscillating, however, between experiencing herself as a single person with multiple facets on the one hand, and as a collection of separate persons who happened to resemble each other and share the same body on the other.

The dream concretizes one phase of this oscillation by replacing the image of four separate boxes with the image of just one that contains four bodies. The patient spontaneously offered the interpretation that the shift from four to one could be understood as a prelude to the integration of her personality, with the exterior boundaries of the final box representing the developing structure of a unitary self. The danger felt to be associated with her impending integration is also concretely symbolized in the dream, by the identification of the box as a coffin. The patient frequently expressed deep anxiety that becoming one would end her life, and she once even suggested that she was coming together as something dead.

The image of the box containing four bodies may also be understood as a symbol of her experience of the therapeutic relationship. The empathic bond, which by this time had become well-established, was exercizing a holding, containing, and integrating function in the patient's efforts to achieve psychological wholeness. Her ambivalence regarding this task emerged quite clearly in the transference, wherein she alternated between embracing her therapist's unifying comprehension and rejecting it as a deadly threat to the survival of the selves. These alternations arose most fundamentally from the patient's deep conviction that she could never fully trust another human being, a conviction that was gradually overcome in stages closely paralleling the integration of her personality.

The dream of the transformation of four boxes into one box buttressed the patient's evolving self-integration by giving her developing unity a concrete form. In the same way that the earlier dream of being burned encapsulated her need to maintain her self-experience as she underwent psychological dissolution, this second dream expressed her need to maintain and consolidate the new but still unsteady structure of integrated self-experience that was gradually crystallizing. An enactment sharing this latter function appeared some nine months after the dream of the boxes. During the interim the patient had continued to wrestle with the problem of unifying herself, with each of the residual fragmentary personalities making a common commitment to a shared future as one individual.

In the subsequent context of such statements as "We are me!" and "I am one now—we voted last night and we all agree," the patient began a therapy session by bringing out twelve small pieces of paper. On six of the slips were written the six names of the part-selves, and on the other six were short phrases designating the pivotal trauma she considered responsible for each of the self-divisions. After asking the therapist whether he thought he could match the selves with their appropriate traumas, she cleared off his desk and assembled out of the twelve pieces of paper two closely juxtaposed columns displaying the temporal sequence of her shattering psychological history. The act of arranging the names and experiences into a single ordered structure clearly concretized the patient's increasingly successful efforts to synthesize an internally integrated, temporally continuous self. By giving the newborn self a tangible form and demonstrating its unity and historical continuity to the therapist, she consolidated the structure of her experience more firmly than had been possible heretofore. Following the integrating enactment involving the twelve pieces of paper, the patient came to feel her own subjective integrity on a consistent basis, and the focus of the therapeutic work shifted to issues other than that of mending her self-fragmentation.

CONCLUSIONS

The basic psychological process that mediates the relationship between experience and action is concretization—the encapsulation of structures of subjectivity by concrete, sensorimotor symbols. After briefly illustrating the role of this process in the creation of neurotic symptoms and symbolic objects, we focused more extensively on two pathways of concretization ubiquitous in human psychological life—enactment and dreaming. While enactments and dreams can be shown to embody multiple personal purposes, a distinctive feature of both is the use of concrete symbolization that serves to crystallize and preserve the organization of the subjective world. Our clinical cases demonstrate that the structure-maintaining function of behavioral enactments and dream imagery can be observed not only when existing structures are threatened, but also when new structures of subjectivity are coming into being and are in need of consolidation. Our cases also show that concretization products such as enactments and dreams cannot be fully comprehended psychoanalytically apart from the intersubjective contexts in which they arise and recede.

5 CONCLUDING REMARKS

We began our project as an attempt to formulate the basic theoretical constructs for a psychoanalytic science of human subjectivity. As we proceeeded with this project, focusing on the structures of personal experiencing as our basic units of analysis, almost unexpectedly two fundamental ideas crystallized out as central principles for a psychoanalytic phenomenology—intersubjectivity and concrete symbolization.

We found the concept of an intersubjective field—a system of differently organized, interacting subjective worlds—to be an invaluable one in illuminating both the vicissitudes of psychoanalytic therapy and the process of human psychological development. This concept can readily be extended to shed light on a wide range of human interactions, including intimate love relationships, family patterns, group processes, and even intergroup relations. The concept of intersubjectivity thus provides a broad basis for a psychoanalytic understanding of human social life, bridging the gap between the analysis of individual subjective worlds and the study of complex social systems. While expanding the scope of psychoanalytic inquiry, the intersubjective viewpoint also enriches the field of social systems analysis.

The concept of concretization—the encapsulation of structures of experience by concrete, sensorimotor symbols—was seen to illuminate a diverse array of psychological phenomena, including neurotic symptoms, symbolic objects, sexual and other enactments, and dreams. This concept, too, can be extended in a number of directions. Extended to the most severe reaches of psychological disorder, it sheds light on the meanings and functions of delusions, hallucinations, and other bizarre symptoms. Extended to shared areas of cultural experience, it enables us to comprehend the significance of artistic creations and ideological symbols. The concretization principle also provides an explanation for the ubiquitous tendency to reify and substantialize the products of human thought, transforming linguistic concepts and abstract ideas into an illusory, symbolic architecture lending concrete substance to organizations of personal, subjective reality. And finally, recognizing the fundamental importance of concrete symbolization in human psychological life brings psychoanalysis into harmony with the contemporary philosophical view (Langer, 1942; Cassirer, 1944) that places symbolizing activity at the heart of what makes human beings distinctively human. By defining itself as a science of human experience, drawing on the rich intellectual heritage of the hermeneutic tradition, phenomenology, and modern structuralism, psychoanalysis discovers its unique and central position among the sciences of man.

REFERENCES

Abraham, K. (1919), A particular form of neurotic resistance against the psycho-analytic method. In: *Selected Papers of Karl Abraham, M.D.* London: Hogarth Press, 1927, pp. 303–311.

Arlow, J. & Brenner, C. (1964), *Psychoanalytic Concepts and the Structural Theory*. New York: International Universities Press.

Atwood, G. (1983), The pursuit of being in the life and thought of Jean-Paul Sartre. *Psychoanal. Rev.*, 70 (in press).

Balint, M. (1969), Trauma and object relations. *Internat. J. Psycho-Anal.*, 50:429–435.

Basch, M. (1977), Developmental psychology and explanatory theory in psychoanalysis. *Ann. Psychoanal.*, 5:229–263.

_____ (in press), Selfobjects and selfobject transference: Theoretical implications. In: *Kohut's Legacy: Contributions to Self Psychology*, ed. A. Goldberg & P. Stepansky. Hillsdale, N.J.: Analytic Press.

Beebe, B. (in press), Mother-infant mutual influence and precursors of self and object representations. In: *Empirical Studies of Psychoanalytic Theories, Vol 2*, ed. J. Masling. Hillsdale, N.J.: Analytic Press.

Binswanger, L. (1963), *Being-in-the-World*. New York: Basic Books.

Boss, M. (1963), *Psychoanalysis and Daseinanalysis*. New York: Basic Books.

_____ (1979), *Existential Foundations of Medicine and Psychology*. New York: Jason Aronson.

Bowlby, J. (1981), Psychoanalysis as a natural science. *Internat. Rev. Psychoanal.*, 8:243–257.

Brandchaft, B. (1983), The negativism of the negative therapeutic reaction and the psychology of the self. In: *The Future of Psychoanalysis*, ed. A. Goldberg, New York: International Universities Press, pp. 327–359.

_____ & Stolorow, R. (1984), The borderline concept: pathological character or iatrogenic myth? In: *Empathy, Volume 2*, ed. J. Lichtenberg, Hillsdale, N.J.: Analytic Press, in press.

121

Breuer, J., & Freud, S. (1893–1895), Studies on hysteria. *Standard Edition, 2.* London: Hogarth Press, 1955.

Cassirer, E. (1944), *An Essay on Man.* New Haven: Yale University Press.

Condon, W., & Sander, L. (1974), Neonate movement is synchronized with adult speech. *Science,* 183:99–101.

Dilthey, W. (1926), *Meaning in History,* ed. H. Rickman. London: Allen & Unwin, 1961.

Duncan, D. (1981), A thought on the nature of psychoanalytic theory. *Internat. J. Psycho-Anal.,* 62:339–349.

Eissler, K. (1958), Notes on problems of technique in the psychoanalytic treatment of adolescents: With some remarks on perversions. *The Psychoanalytic Study of the Child,* 13:223–254. New York: International Universities Press.

Erikson, E. (1950), *Childhood and Society.* New York: Norton.

———— (1954), The dream specimen of psychoanalysis. *J. Amer. Psychoanal. Assn.,* 2:5–56.

———— (1956), The problem of ego identity. In: *Identity and the Life Cycle (Psychological Issues,* Monogr. 1). New York; International Universities Press, 1959, pp. 101–171.

Fenichel, O. (1941), *Problems of Psychoanalytic Technique.* New York: Psychoanalytic Quarterly, Inc.

Fosshage, J. (1983), The psychological function of dreams: A revised psychoanalytic perspective. *Psychoanal. & Contemp. Thought,* in press.

French, T., & Fromm, E. (1964), *Dream Interpretation: A New Approach.* New York: Basic Books.

Freud, S. (1900), The interpretation of dreams. *Standard Edition,* 4 & 5. London: Hogarth Press, 1953.

———— (1905), Three essays on the theory of sexuality. *Standard Edition,* 7:125–243. London: Hogarth Press, 1953.

———— (1914), Remembering, repeating and working through. *Standard Edition,* 12:146–156. London: Hogarth Press, 1958.

———— (1919), Lines of advance in psychoanalytic therapy. *Standard Edition,* 17:157–168. London: Hogarth Press, 1955.

———— (1923), The ego and the id. *Standard Edition,* 19:3–66. London: Hogarth Press, 1961.

———— (1924), The dissolution of the oedipus complex. *Standard Edition,* 19:173–179. London: Hogarth Press, 1961.

———— (1937), Analysis terminable and interminable. *Standard Edition,* 23:211–253. London: Hogarth Press, 1964.

Gadamer, H. (1975), *Truth and method.* New York: Seabury Press.

Gallie, W. (1974), *Philosophy and the Historical Understanding.* New York: Schocken Books.

Goldberg, A. (1975), A fresh look at perverse behavior. *Internat. J. Psycho-Anal.,* 56:335–342.

Greenson, R. (1967), *The Technique and Practice of Psychoanalysis.* New York: International Universities Press.

Greenspan, S. (1979), *Intelligence and Adaptation.* New York: International Universities Press.

Guntrip, H. (1967), The concept of psychodynamic science. *Internat. J. Psycho-Anal.,* 48:32–43.

Hanly, C. (1979), *Psychoanalysis and Existentialism.* New York: International

Universities Press.

Hartmann, H. (1939), *Ego Psychology and the Problem of Adaptation.* New York: International Universities Press, 1958.

Heidegger, M. (1927), *Being and Time.* New York: Harper & Row, 1962.

Hoffer, W. (1950), Development of the body ego. *The Psychoanalytic Study of the Child,* 5:18–23. New York: International Universities Press.

Husserl, E. (1931), *Ideas: An Introduction to Pure Phenomenology.* New York: Macmillan.

––––– (1936), *The Crisis of European Sciences and Transcendental Phenomenology.* Evanston: Northwestern University Press, 1970.

Jacobson, E. (1964), *The Self and the Object World.* New York: International Universities Press.

Kernberg, O. (1975), *Borderline Conditions and Pathological Narcissism.* New York: Jason Aronson.

––––– (1976), *Object Relations Theory and Clinical Psychoanalysis.* New York: Jason Aronson.

Klein, M. (1957), *Envy and Gratitude.* New York: Basic Books.

Klein, G. (1976). *Psychoanalytic Theory.* New York: International Universities Press.

Kohut, H. (1959), Introspection, empathy,and psychoanalysis: An examination of the relationship between mode of observation and theory. In: *The Search for the Self,* ed. P. Ornstein. New York: International Universities Press, 1978, pp. 205–232.

––––– (1971), *The Analysis of the Self.* New York: International Universities Press.

––––– (1977), *The Restoration of the Self.* New York: International Universities Press.

––––– (1983), Selected problems of self-psychological theory. In: *Reflections on Self Psychology,* ed. J. Lichtenberg & S. Kaplan. Hillsdale, N.J.: Analytic Press, in press.

Lacan, J. (1953), The function and field of speech and language in psychoanalysis. In: *Ecrits.* New York: Norton, 1977, pp. 30–113.

––––– (1958), The direction of the treatment and the principles of its power. In: *Ecrits.* New York: Norton, 1977, pp. 226–280.

Langer, S. (1942), *Philosophy in a New Key.* Cambridge: Harvard University Press.

Leavy, S. (1980), *The Psychoanalytic Dialogue.* New Haven: Yale University Press.

Lerner, B. (1967), Dream function reconsidered. *J. Abnorm. Psychol.,* 72:85–100.

Levi-Strauss, C. (1963), *Structural Anthropology.* New York: Basic Books.

Lichtenberg, J. (1975), The development of the sense of self. *J. Amer. Psychoanal. Assn.,* 23:453–484.

––––– (1978), Transmuting internalization and developmental change. Presented at Chicago Conference on the Psychology of the Self, October.

––––– (1981), Implications for psychoanalytic theory of research on the neonate. *Internat. Rev. Psycho-Anal.,* 8:35–52.

Lichtenstein, H. (1961), Identity and sexuality: A study of their interrelationship in man. *J. Amer. Psychoanal. Assn.,* 9:179–260.

Loewald, H. (1960), On the therapeutic action of psychoanalysis. *Internat. J. Psycho-Anal.,* 41:16–33.

———— (1970), Psychoanalytic theory and the psychoanalytic process. *The Psychoanalytic Study of the Child,* 25:45–68. New York: International Universities Press.

———— (1978), *Psychoanalysis and the History of the Individual.* New Haven: Yale University Press.

Mahler, M. (1968), *On Human Symbiosis and the Vicissitudes of Individuation.* New York: International Universities Press.

———— Pine, F., & Bergman, A. (1975), *The Psychological Birth of the Human Infant.* New York: Basic Books.

Makkreel, R. (1975), *Dilthey: Philosopher of the Human Studies.* Princeton: Princeton University Press.

May, R., Angel, E., & Ellenberger, H. (1958), *Existence.* New York: Basic Books.

Miller, A. (1979), *Prisoners of Childhood.* New York: Basic Books, 1981.

Modell, A. (1976), The "holding environment" and the therapeutic action of psychoanalysis. *J. Amer. Psychoanal. Assn.,* 24:285–307.

Monchaux, C. de (1978), Dreaming and the organizing function of the ego. *Internat. J. Psycho-Anal.,* 59:443–453.

Nydes, J. (1950), The magical experience of the masturbation fantasy. *Amer. J. Psychother.,* 4:303–310.

Palmer, R. (1969), *Hermeneutics: Interpretation Theory in Schleiermacher, Dilthey, Heidegger, and Gadamer.* Evanston: Northwestern University Press.

Perls, F. (1969), *In and Out the Garbage Pail.* Moab, Utah: Real People Press.

Piaget, J. (1970a), *The Place of the Sciences of Man in the System of Sciences.* New York: Harber & Row, 1974.

———— (1970b), *Structuralism.* New York: Basic Books.

———— (1972), *The Child and Reality.* New York: Viking Press, 1973.

Ricouer, P. (1970), *Freud and Philosophy.* New Haven: Yale University Press.

———— (1974), The question of proof in Freud's psychoanalytic writings. *J. Amer. Psychoanal. Assn.,* 25:835–871.

Riviere, J. (1936), A contribution to the analysis of the negative therapeutic reaction. *Internat. J. Psycho-Anal.,* 17:304–320.

Sander, L. (1975), Infant and caretaking environment: Investigation and conceptualization of adaptive behavior in a system of increasing complexity. In: *Explorations in Child Psychiatry,* ed. E. J. Anthony. New York: Plenum Press, p. 147.

———— (1976), Epilogue. In: *Infant Psychiatry: A New Synthesis,* ed. E. Rexford et al. New Haven: Yale University Press.

———— (1977), The regulation of exchange in the infant-caretaker system and some aspects of the context-content relationship. In: *Interaction, Conversation, and the Development of Language,* ed. M. Lewis & L. Rosenblum, New York: Wiley, pp. 133–156.

Sandler, J., & Sandler, A.-M. (1978), On the development of object relationships and affects. *Internat. J. Psycho-Anal.,* 59:285–296.

Sartre, J.-P. (1943), *Being and Nothingness.* New York: Washington Square Press, 1966.

———— (1946), *No Exit.* New York: Knopf, 1947.

———— (1964), *The Words.* New York: Braziller.

Schafer, R. (1976), *A New Language for Psychoanalysis.* New Haven: Yale University Press.

Schwaber, E. (1979), On the 'self' within the matrix of analytic theory—some clinical reflections and reconsiderations. *Internat. J. Psycho-Anal.*, 60:467–479.

Sherwood, M. (1969), *The Logic of Explanation in Psychoanalysis.* New York: Academic Press.

Slap, J., & Saykin, A. (1980), The schema: Basic concept in a nonmetapsychological model of the mind. Presented at meeting of the American Psychoanalytic Association, New York, December.

Socarides, C. (1978), *Homosexuality.* New York: Jason Aronson.

———— (1980), Perverse symptoms and the manifest dream of perversion. In: *The Dream in Clinical Practice,* ed. J. Natterson. New York: Jason Aronson, pp. 237–256.

Spence, D. (1982), *Narrative Truth and Historical Truth.* New York: Norton.

Spiegelberg, H. (1976), *The Phenomenological Movement.* The Hague: Martinus Nijhoff.

Spitz, R. (1964), The derailment of dialogue. *J. Amer. Psychoanal. Assn.,* 12:752–775.

Steele, R. (1979), Psychoanalysis and hermeneutics. *Internat. Rev. Psycho-Anal.,* 6:389–411.

Stern, D. (1971), A microanalysis of mother-infant interaction. *J. Amer. Acad. Child Psychiat.,* 10:501–517.

———— (1983), The early development of schemas of self, of other, and of various experiences of "self with other." In: *Reflections on Self Psychology,* ed. J. Lichtenberg & S. Kaplan. Hillsdale, N.J.: Analytic Press.

Stolorow, R. (1978), Themes in dreams: A brief contribution to therapeutic technique. *Internat. J. Psycho-Anal.,* 59:473–475.

———— (1979), Psychosexuality and the representational world. *Internat. J. Psycho-Anal.,* 60:39–45.

———— & Atwood, G. (1979), *Faces in a Cloud: Subjectivity in Personality Theory.* New York: Jason Aronson.

———— ———— & Lachmann, F. (1981), Transference and countertransference in the analysis of developmental arrests. *Bull. Menninger Clinic,* 45:20–28.

———— ———— & Ross, J. (1978), The representational world in psychoanalytic therapy. *Internat. Rev. Psycho-Anal.,* 5:247–256.

———— Brandchaft, B., & Atwood, G. (1983), Intersubjectivity in psychoanalytic treatment: With special reference to archaic states. *Bull. Menninger Clinic,* 47:117–128.

———— & Lachmann, F. (1980), *Psychoanalysis of Developmental Arrests: Theory and Treatment.* New York: International Universities Press.

Stone, L. (1961), *The Psychoanalytic Situation.* New York: International Universities Press.

Strachey, J. (1934), The nature of the therapeutic action of psychoanalysis. *Internat. J. Psycho-Anal.,* 15:127–159.

Sullivan, H. S. (1953), *Interpersonal Theory of Psychiatry.* New York: Norton.

Viderman, S. (1974), Interpretation in the analytical space. *Internat. Rev. Psycho-Anal.,* 1:467–480.

Waelder, R. (1936), The principle of multiple function: Observations on overdetermination. *Psychoanal. Quart.,* 5:45–62.

Winnicott, D. (1951), Transitional objects and transitional phenomena. In: *Though Paediatrics to Psycho-Analysis.* New York: Basic Books, 1975, pp. 229–242.

———— (1960), Ego distortion in terms of true and false self. In: *The Maturational Processes and the Facilitating Environment.* New York: International Universities Press, 1965, pp. 140–152.

———— (1965), *The Maturational Processes and the Facilitating Environment.* New York: International Universities Press.

Wolf, E. (1980), On the developmental line of selfobject relations. In: *Advances in Self Psychology,* ed. A. Goldberg. New York: International Universities Press, pp. 117–130.

Author Index

A

Abraham, K., 52, *121*
Angel, E., 31, *124*
Arlow, J., 103, *121*
Atwood, G., 29, 36, 37, 41, 42, 46, 49, 52, 60,
  87, 91, *121, 125*

B

Balint, M., 45, *121*
Basch, M., 37, 68, *121*
Beebe, B., 67, *121*
Bergman, A., 37, 71, 92, *124*
Binswanger, L., 31, *121*
Boss, M., 31, *121*
Bowlby, J., 66, *121*
Brandchaft, B., 41, 52, 55, *121, 125*
Brenner, C., 103, *121*
Breuer, J., 86, *122*

C

Cassirer, E., 120, *122*
Condon, W., 67, *122*

D

de Monchaux, C., 103, *124*
Dilthey, W., 2, 3, *122*
Duncan, D., 5, *122*

E

Eissler, K., 94, *122*
Ellenberger, H., 31, *124*
Erikson, E., 38, 66, 93, 98, *122*

F

Fenichel, O., 46, *122*
Fosshage, J., 103, *122*
Freud, S., 44, 52, 59, 71, 86, 94, 97, 99, 101,
  103, *122*
French, T., 103, *122*
Fromm, E., 103, *122*

G

Gadamer, H., 3, *122*
Gallie, W., 6, *122*
Goldberg, A., 94, *122*
Greenson, R., 45, *122*
Greenspan, S., 37, *122*
Guntrip, H., 4, *122*

H

Hanly, C., 30, *123*
Hartmann, H., 66, *123*
Heidegger, M., 15, *123*
Hoffer, W., 92, *123*
Husserl, E., 9, 12, *123*

J

Jacobson, E., 37, 38, *123*

K

Kernberg, O., 38, 52, 71, *123*
Klein, G., 4, 34, 35, 101, *123*
Klein, M., 52, *123*
Kohut, H., 4, 34, 37, 38, 40, 41, 45, 52, 56,
  61, 62, 67, 68, 71, 79, 93, 94, 97, 104, *123*

L

Lacan, J., 4, 5, 36, 87, *123*
Lachmann, F., 37, 40, 45, 52, 61, 62, 88, 92,
  93, 94, 95, *125*
Langer, S., 120, *123*
Leavy, S., 4, 5, *123*
Lerner, B., 103, *123*
Levi-Strauss, C., 36, *123*
Lichtenberg, J., 38, 62, 67, *123*
Lichtenstein, H., 66, 69, *123*
Loewald, H., 45, 59, 65, 67, *123, 124*

M

Mahler, M., 37, 66, 71, 92, *124*
Makkreel, R., 2, *124*
May, R., 31, *124*
Miller, A., 69, 90, *124*
Modell, A., 45, *124*

N

Nydes, J., 94, *124*

P

Palmer, R., 3, *124*
Perls, F., 48, *124*

Piaget, J., 34, 36, 47, *124*
Pine, F., 37, 71, 92, *124*

R

Ricouer, P., 4, 6, *124*
Riviere, J., 52, *124*
Ross, J., 60, *125*

S

Sander, L., 65, 67, *122, 124*
Sandler, A. M., 34, 91, *124*
Sandler, J., 34, 91, *124*
Sartre, J.-P., 23, 28, 29, *124*
Saykin, A., 34, *125*
Schafer, R., 4, 35, *124*
Schwaber, E., 41, 68, *125*
Sherwood, M., 4, 6, *125*
Slap, J., 34, *125*
Socarides, C., 94, 104, *125*
Spence, D., 7, *125*
Spiegelberg, H., 13, 14, 15, *125*
Spitz, R., 67, *125*
Steele, R., 4, *125*
Stern, D., 67, *125*
Stolorow, R., 36, 37, 40, 41, 42, 45, 46, 49,
  52, 55, 60, 61, 62, 87, 88, 91, 92, 93, 94, 95,
  99, *121, 125*
Stone, L., 45, *125*
Strachey, J., 59, *125*
Sullivan, H. S., 67, *125*

V

Viderman, S., 6, *125*

W

Waddington, 66
Waelder, R., 46, 103, *125*
Winnicott, D., 45, 65, 69, 88, 113, *125, 126*
Wolf, E., 68, *118*

Subject Index

A

Abstinence
  concept of, 44–45
  negative therapeutic reaction to, 53–54
Affectively discrepant experiences,
  integration of, 76–79
Alienation, 21–23
Anal-retentive mode, 93
Anguish, flight from, 25–26
Anonymity of therapist, 45
Anxiety, Heidegger's concept of, 19–21
Archaic bonds, 56–59, 61, 113
Archaic narcissism, 58
"As-if personality," 30
Authenticity, death and, 19–20
Autonomy
  surrender of, 19
  of transcendental ego, 13–15

B

Bad faith, attitude of, 26
Behavioral enactments. See Enactments
Being, nature of
  Heidegger's explorations of, 15–23
  Sartre's categories of, 23–30
Being and Nothingness (Sartre), 23–28
Being and Time (Heidegger), 15–23
Borderline psychopathology, 55–56

C

"Call of conscience," 21–22
Care, attitude of, 17–18
Case study, psychoanalytic, 4–7
Causal analysis, 32–33
Character, concept of, 34, 91
Clinical theory, 101–102
Concretization, 85–117
  concept of, 119–120
  defined, 85
  in dreams, 97–116
    concrete symbolization in, 101–116
    nature of interpretation of, 98–101
  enactments, 91–97
  neurotic symptoms, 86–88
  symbolic objects, 88–91
Condensation, mechanism of, 99–100
Conduct, pattern of, 91–92
Conjunction, intersubjective, 47–52
"Conscience, call of," 21–22
Consciousness
  essential feature of, 27
  in Husserlian philosophy, 14–15
  Sartre's ontology of, 23–30
Constancy of identity, 19
  object and self, 38
Contextualism, subjective, 35
Countertransference, 47–52
  consequences of, 50–52

defined, 47
negative therapeutic reaction and, 54

D

"Dasein" (being-there), 16–23
Death, authenticity and, 19–20
Defenses, 35–36
Depression, post-partum, 70
Development. *See under* Intersubjectivity
Differentiation, self-object, 37–38, 71–75, 93
Disjunction, intersubjective, 47–52
negative thereapeutic reactions and, 52–55
Displacement, mechanism of, 100
Dreams, 97–116
concrete symbolization in, 101–116
organization of experience and, 102–105
nature of interpretation of, 98–101
Dynamic unconscious, 35–36

E

Ego, transcendental, 10–13
authenticity of, 13–15
Empathy, 4–5
bond of, 113, 115
mutative power of, 61–62
Enactments
concretization through, 91–97, 104, 116
of fragmented personality, 107–113, 116
Epoche, 9–15
"Existentialia" of Heidegger, 17
Existential phenomenology, 7–31
Heidegger's contributions to, 15–23
Husserlian system of, 8–15
Sartre's philosophy of, 23–30
Experience
affectively discrepant, 76–79
organization of, 35–36, 114
in dreams, 102–105
negative organizing principle, 35
sensual, 92–95
structuralization of, 33–34, 36–39

F

Falling into inauthenticity, 19–22
Fragmentation of personality, 78–79, 105–116
Frame of reference, abstinence principle and, 45

Free-association, 42–44
dream interpretation and, 99
resistance to, 43
Freedom
loss of, 27–29
Sartrean doctrine of, 25

G

Genital modes, 93

H

Heidegger, Martin, 15–23
"Hermeneutic circle," 3, 5
Hermeneutics, 2–7
dream interpretation and, 99–101
History, philosophy of, 2–3
Homosexual patterns, 94–96
Husserl, Edmund, 8–15

I

Identity, constancy of, 19
object and self, 38
Inauthenticity, falling into, 19–22
Infant-mother relations, 66–71
Integration, 37–38
of affectively discrepant experiences, 76–79
"Interactionist" perspective, 66–67
Interferences with treatment, 48–52
Internalization
of analyst's observational stance, 61, 62
transmuting, 39
Interpretation
of dreams, 98–101
rules of, 45–46
Interpretation of Dreams, The (Freud), 101–102
Intersubjectivity, 5, 41–84
concept of, 119
dependence of psychoanalytic insight on, 6
development and pathogenesis, 36–39, 65–84
integration of affectively discrepant experiences, 76–79
oedipal phase, 79–83
self-object differentiation, 37–38, 71–75, 93
Husserl's formulation of, 11
in therapeutic situation, 41–64

establishing relationship, 112–114
negative therapeutic reactions, 52–55
psychoanalytic situation, 42–46
psychopathology, 39–40, 55–59
therapeutic action, 59–63
Invariance, 33

J

Jung, Carl, 90–91

M

Masochistic perversion, 95
Metapsychology, 30–31, 101–102
Misunderstanding, 50–52
    enactments in response to, 113–114
    negative therapeutic reactions due to,
        52–54
Motivation, 35
Mutual regulation, 66–70

N

Narcissism, archaic, 58
Negative organizing principle, 35
Negative therapeutic reactions, 52–55
Neurotic symptoms, 86–88
Neutrality of therapist, 44–45
    negative therapeutic reaction to, 53–54
No Exit (Sartre), 28–29
Nothingness, concept of, 24–27

O

"Object constancy," 38
"Objectness," 27–29
Observational stance, 61–62, 65–66, 83
Oedipal period, passage through, 79–83
Ontology
    of consciousness, 23–30
    Heidegger's investigation of, 16–23
Oral-incorporative mode, 93
Organization of experience, 35–36, 114
    in dreams, 102–105
    negative organizing principle, 35
    See also Structuralization

P

Paranoid transference psychosis, 57–58
Pathogenesis. See under Intersubjectivity

Pathological structures
    psychological health and, 39–40
    structural transformation of, 60–63
Personality
    "as-if," 30
    development, 36–39, 65–83
        integration of affectively discrepant
            experiences, 76–79
        oedipal phase, 79–83
        self-object differentiation, 37–38, 71–75,
            93
    fragmentation of, 105–116
    structure, 33–34
Perverse enactments, 94–97, 104
Phenomenology, existential. See Existential
    phenomenology
Phenomenology, psychoanalytic. See
    Psychoanalytic phenomenology,
    philosophical context of
Post-partum depression, 70
Prediction, in causal analysis, 32–33
Premature ejaculation, case study of, 80–83
Prereflective unconscious, 36, 42, 98–99
Psychoanalytic case study, 4–7
Psychoanalytic phenomenology,
        philosophical contest of, 1–40
    existential phenomenology and, 7–31
        Heidegger's contributions to, 15–23
        Husserlian system of, 8–15
        Sartre's philosophy of, 23–30
    hermeneutic tradition of, 2–7
    structuralism and, 31–40
        invariance in, 33
        method of analysis, 31–32
        motivation, 35
        personality development, 36–39
        personality structure, 33–34
        psychological health and pathology,
            39–40
        repression and the unconscious, 35–36
Psychoanalytic situation, 42–46
Psychological health, 39–40
Psychopathology, 55–59
    borderline, 55–56
    classes of, 39–40
Psychosis, transference, 57–59

R

Radical freedom, doctrine of, 25, 30
Reduction, phenomenological, 9–15

Regulation, mutual, 66–70
Reification, 7, 27
Relatedness
  archaic, 113
  attitude of care, 17–18
Repression, 35–36
Resistance analysis, 63

S

Sartre, Jean-Paul, 23–30
  treatment of social relationships, 27–29
Self, concept of, 34
Self-awareness of analyst, 47–48, 58
Self-boundaries, formation of, 71–75
"Self constancy," 38
Selfobject
  concept, 68–70
  defined, 39
  transference, 52–54, 56, 61–63, 69, 97
Self-object differentiation, 37–38, 71–75, 93
"Self-state dreams," 104–105
Sensual experiences, 92–95
Sexual enactments, 92–97, 104
Social relationships, Sartre's treatment of, 27–29
Structuralism, 31–40
  invariance in, 33
  method of analysis, 31–32
  motivation, 35
  personality
    development, 36–39
    structure, 33–34
  psychological health and pathology, 39–40
  repression and the unconscious, 35–36
Structuralization
  of experience, 33–34, 36–39
  faulty, 40, 60
  optimal, 39
  See also Organization of experience
Structural transformation, 60–63

Subjective contextualism, 35
Subjectivity, transcendental, 10–11
Symbolic objects, 88–91
Symbolization
  concrete, 101–116
  unconscious, 86–88

T

Therapeutic situation, 41–64
  establishing relationship, 112–114
  negative therapeutic reactions, 52–55
  psychoanalytic situation, 42–46
  psychopathology, 39–40, 55–59
  therapeutic action, 59–63
  countertransference, 47–52
  See also Transference
"Thrownness," 18
Transcendental ego, 10–13
  autonomy of, 13–15
Transcendental phenomenology, 9–15
Transference, 6, 47–52
  concept of, 47
  consequences of, 48–50
  development of, 44
  integrative capacity and, 77–79
  psychosis, 57–59
  selfobject, 52–54, 56, 61–63, 69, 97
Transitional object, 88–89
Transmuting internalization, 39

U

Unconscious, the
  prereflective, 36, 42, 98–99
  repression and, 35–36
Unconscious symbolization, 86–88

W

Wish fulfillment in dreams, 100